THE
SEDGEFORD
HOARD

Pat Chapman, Gareth Davies, Megan Dennis, Neil Faulkner, Val Fryer,
Martin Hatton, Chris Mackie, Ray Thirkettle and Liz Wilson.
2004

Sedgeford Historical and Archaeological Research Project

THE
SEDGEFORD
HOARD

MEGAN DENNIS and NEIL FAULKNER

TEMPUS

This book is dedicated to the memory of Dr Hugh Ford CVO (1929-2004), inaugural chairperson of SHARP (1996-2002).

First published 2005

Tempus Publishing Limited
The Mill, Brimscombe Port,
Stroud, Gloucestershire, GL5 2QG
www.tempus-publishing.com

British Library Cataloguing in Publication Data.
A catalogue record for this book is available from the British Library.

ISBN 0 7524 3438 1

Typesetting and origination by Tempus Publishing Limited
Printed in Great Britain

CONTENTS

Sedgeford

Now it is Summertime,
And the sun's hot breath
Sucks 'precious' moisture from the clay,
Silently as a dry mime
Behind a mummer's dead eyes.

Now it is Summertime:
Here in this field of decay and death,
Shining brightly as the day
Came forth a hoard, a herd of history's wealth.
From the 'Boneyard's' ancient slime.

Through fate a cow's bone yields
By the hand of villainy or mischance
Glittering, coins from a 'darker' time!
Now it is Summertime
Here in these Norfolk fields

Golden horses lightly, gaily prance.
Out of the 'Boneyard's' bloodrich earth.
Come the joyous sounds of mirth.
Now it is eventime
Far beyond our golden sleep

Pegasus rises on triumphant wings
A silent watch to keep
Upon the golden herd.
Sedgeford, the twelfth day of August in the Year of
Our hoard Two Thousand & Three.

James Riches, SHARP volunteer

FOREWORD

On 12 August 2003, at Sedgeford in north-west Norfolk (*1*), archaeologists excavated a cow bone containing 20 Iron Age gold coins. Eight other coins of similar type had been found nearby in previous years, and a further 11 were found scattered in the soil around the bone, bringing the total for the hoard to at least 39 (with the probability that others had been recovered before the archaeological excavation).

It is rare for hoards to be recovered by archaeologists. Most treasure finds nowadays are made by metal-detectorists. Even when archaeologists do excavate treasure, it is usually in the context of a rescue dig, sometimes one that has been organised in response to an accidental discovery. It is very rare for archaeologists to excavate treasure in the context of a research project like that at Sedgeford.

The Sedgeford Historical and Archaeological Research Project (SHARP) was set up in 1995 to investigate the history of settlement and land-use in a fairly ordinary English parish. Our main focus to date has been the origins and early development of the medieval village located near the middle of the parish, but excavation and field surveys have, over the years, yielded evidence for a strong Iron Age presence. In particular, on the main excavation site, Boneyard-Reeddam, where we are digging an Anglo-Saxon settlement and cemetery, we have long been aware of Iron Age deposits beneath (*2*).

Not only is SHARP a long-term field research project, it is also an experiment in what we call 'archaeology from below' or 'democratic archaeology' – that is, archaeology rooted in the community, open to volunteer contributions, organised in an inclusive way and working to a flexible, open-ended research agenda in which material (what we dig up), methods (how we

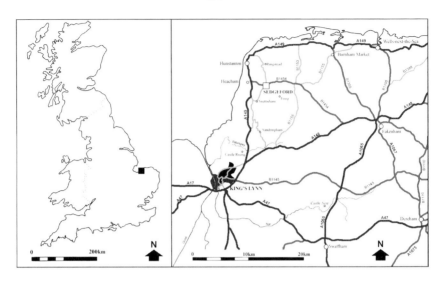

1 The location of Sedgeford in north–west Norfolk. *Illustration by Andrea Cox, reproduced from Ordnance Survey based mapping on behalf of Her Majesty's Stationery Office © Crown Copyright 100043498 2004*

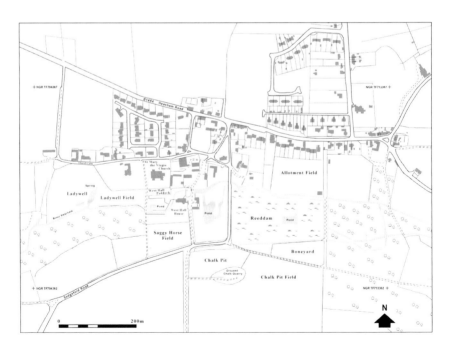

2 The location of the Boneyard-Reeddam site, where the hoard was found, near the modern village of Sedgeford. *Illustration by Andrea Cox, reproduced from Ordnance Survey based mapping on behalf of Her Majesty's Stationery Office © Crown Copyright 100043498 2004*

dig it) and meanings (what we make of it all) interact and influence one another. This is very different from most archaeology today, where professional units, operating on a commercial basis, work to strict 'project designs', and are organised in traditional hierarchies with decision-making power concentrated at the top.

The Sedgeford hoard was, therefore, important for two reasons: it was a treasure find that could be put in context because it was excavated carefully as part of a wider research project; and it was recovered by a team of volunteer excavators working on a project concerned with democratising archaeology and maximising access. In order to continue this open access policy, we decided to publish this short book as quickly as possible.

Chapter one describes the discovery, excavation and public presentation of the hoard, mainly in the words of those involved. Its purpose is to illustrate the degree to which ordinary people have direct personal access to the archaeology at Sedgeford, and to introduce some of the public archaeology issues discussed in a more theoretical way in chapter six. Chapter two provides a full description and analysis of the hoard itself, while chapter three deals with the excavation of the hoard pit and its immediate archaeological context. Chapter four discusses the hoard in relation to Iron Age archaeology in the region, in the rest of Britain and on the Continent. Chapter five offers a range of comments on the interpretation and significance of the Sedgeford hoard. Chapter six explores the relationship between archaeology, treasure and the community.

A general caveat must be entered: field work, analysis of finds and the interpretation of data are ongoing. We have tried to indicate degrees of certainty about statements we make in the text. We have sometimes included alternative interpretations side-by-side. But even where we make apparently unqualified assertions, they should be read critically: new discoveries and clearer thinking may yet dissolve them.

Like the project, the monograph is the product of many contributions – in the field, the lab and the study. In a sense, everyone who has been part of the project has helped, however indirectly, to make the monograph possible. More specifically, the 2003 supervisory team rallied round to facilitate the work of colleagues involved with the hoard. Among those working hard in the background so that others could be in the limelight were Bill Armitage, Zannah Baldry, Terry Baxter, Charlotte Burrill, Sophie Cabot, Stuart Calow, Jon Cousins, Anj Cox, Nicky Dennies, Sally Faulkner, Hugh Ford, Val Fryer, Sarah Glover, Martin Hatton, Matt Hobson, Holly Holman, Chris Kelly, Ray

Ludford, Claire Malleson, Wendy Martin, Anthony Maynard, Jean McGinty, Gabe Moshenska, Naomi Payne, Jim Reid, Pat Reid, Kelvin Smith, Hilary Snelling, Tim Snelling, Helen Thirkettle and Ray Thirkettle. Because of this team's commitment, our hoard 'specialists' were able to carry out the work on which this short monograph is based. Megan Dennis, the director of Iron Age research at SHARP, co-ordinated the hoard project as a whole, was the author of chapter two, joint author of chapter four and was the principal editor of this monograph. Pat Chapman, SHARP finds supervisor, and Chris Mackie, the SHARP director responsible for public relations, played major roles in, respectively, finds processing and publicity, and they jointly collated chapters one and five. Gareth Davies, the director of Old Trench excavation, personally supervised the investigation of the hoard pit and is therefore the principal author of chapter three. Liz Wilson, formerly a SHARP supervisor and now Finds Liaison Officer for Sussex, was the joint author with Megan of chapter four. Finally, as SHARP's founder-director, I wrote chapter six and helped edit the final text.

Neil Faulkner
April 2004

ONE

DISCOVERY

It was close to the end of the summer digging season. Parts of the excavation were already being shut down for the winter. Terry Baxter, SHARP site supervisor, and Kev Woodward, RAF engineer, veteran metal-detectorist and regular SHARP volunteer, were doing a final metal-detector sweep over their area. It was the boggy part of Boneyard-Reeddam, where Old Trench excavation extended from the bottom of the hill out into the flat marsh. The excavation here was unfinished – it would have to be continued next year – and they needed to check for metal finds near the surface. If the archaeologists did not recover them, the nighthawks (illicit metal-detector users who steal archaeological finds for profit) would be likely to get them.

Terry Baxter, SHARP supervisor:

> We got a signal. After clearing the area, we found it was a buried scaffolding plank from the previous year, the signal coming from the metal binding on the end. Moving along, Kev got another signal – probably a submerged angle-iron fence post like the one still standing on the edge of the excavation. We dug.

Kev Woodward, SHARP volunteer:

> Once it became clear the signal came from beneath the unexplored archaeological layer, our attitude changed. The machine indicated it was non-

ferrous and 14 inches long. Terry removed two inches of soil with his trowel, and then I swept the area again. The signal had not changed, so more soil was removed. Two inches more down and I came across an animal bone lying on its side. I lifted the bone and dug some more. Once Terry and I had cleaned the area up, I swept over the hole again. This time things were different, and my mind went into overdrive: there were signals coming from both our little heaps of spoil and from the hole itself – lots of them. Within a few seconds I had an Iron Age gold coin in my quivering hand, and within a minute we had recovered four more identical coins from the spoil heaps. There were still signals from the hole, so I moved the detector-head away so that Terry could continue the excavation. In doing so, I passed it over the animal bone, and the detector gave off a strong signal. To investigate this, I moved the bone, assuming it was in the way, but when I tried again the signal had disappeared. Only then did it dawn on me that maybe a coin had got lodged inside the bone, so I passed the detector-head over it and received a strong signal. I carefully picked out some of the mud inside the broken end of the shaft. Two gold coins appeared, wedged inside. It was then that I noticed how heavy the bone was. And, as I tilted it, I could feel more coins moving around inside ….

Kev struggled for words. He and Terry were soon shaking with emotion. Others were alerted to the discovery, digging was suspended and the bone and loose coins were taken to the Finds Hut. The news spread rapidly across the site.

Chris Mackie, SHARP director:

Clearly, with so many volunteers and visitors on site, we were not going to be able to keep the lid on the news. It was decision time. First off, we needed an X-ray of the bone, so I called the Norfolk Museums Service, but they could not help. I went into King's Lynn and eventually ended up at the Sandringham Hospital, where the radiologists agreed to X-ray the bone within minutes of my arrival. It is difficult to express my feelings when I saw the images come up on the screen. We had a hoard of gold. On an X-ray video shot, I thought I could count 20 coins … (3)

Chris was back at the site by lunchtime. The X-rays caused a sensation. They also contributed to a growing sense of crisis: with only a few days in the field left, as well as dealing with the hoard itself, it would be necessary to complete a thorough archaeological investigation of the find-spot to ensure that

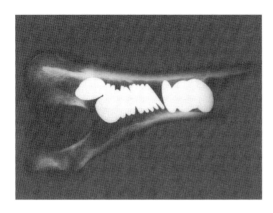

3 Twenty gold coins in a cow bone? The X-ray of the hoard bone before the coins were removed. *Courtesy of Sandringham Hospital*

4 SHARP volunteers pan for gold. Every bucket of soil removed from the excavation of the hoard site was wet-sieved to recover all artefacts. *Photograph by Terry Baxter*

nothing remained for the nighthawks. Gareth Davies, Old Trench director, set up a meticulous, spit-by-spit excavation of the area, and the archaeo-environmental team wet-sieved every bucket of soil that came out (*4*).

Kev Woodward, SHARP volunteer:

> I remember the screams of delight when, on separate occasions, two more coins were found at the wet-sieving station. We worked until the light faded, removing layer by layer the soil from around and on top of the find-spot. Everything was drawn, photographed and recorded at each stage. That first night, the drawing was finished by torch-light.

By coincidence, on the same day, another spectacular discovery had been made higher up the slope in Old Trench: the burial of a horse in a pit close to the end of a huge ditch. It was found in levels well below the Anglo-Saxon. There was a sherd of Gallo-Belgic type pottery overlying the skull. It was, therefore, almost certainly also Iron Age. (*colour plate 1*)

Helen Thirkettle, SHARP supervisor:

> The burial was discovered with that delicate archaeological tool the mattock, which sliced through the forelimbs. Trowelling revealed not the expected rubbish dump, but the articulated vertebrae of a large animal. As one of the site's animal-bone specialists, I was invited to confirm the suspicion that the spine belonged to a horse – which, to my delight, it did. Pegasus (as he was quickly named) had the teeth of a male of about 8-10 years. The neck had been deliberately twisted back on itself, so the horse was 'looking over its shoulder', and there seemed to be damage to the skull.

Two immediate issues were the stability of the cow-bone 'money box' – now removed from its damp environment – and the security of the gold coins. Archaeologists often improvise. Mostly, everyday equipment is derived from other crafts. Dealing with the unexpected, they use what comes to hand.

Chris Mackie, SHARP director:

> Pat Chapman took charge of the loose coins, and I took the bone home with me. It was moist but in danger of cracking if it dried out too quickly,

and if the soil inside had dried and hardened, the coins would have been more difficult to excavate. I had a small Coca Cola cool-bag. It was an almost perfect temporary home for the bone. I made a bed of bubble wrap with, on top, a layer of acid-free paper moistened with distilled water. The cool-bag was easy to carry, it was padded and it kept its contents cool and damp.

WEDNESDAY 13 AUGUST 2003

Rebecca Ferrugia, SHARP volunteer:

We were back on site at 6am the next day, excavating close to the actual find-spot. The deposit was hard to dig because of tree roots. I spent an hour battling with roots and finding nothing, not even a small fragment of bone or pot – when suddenly out popped a gold coin. That is something I will never forget. Being present when the hoard was found and then finding a gold coin myself was a truly fantastic experience. Most thrilling was knowing that we were the first people to hold those coins since they were buried.

5 The hoard hits the headlines. Cole Green Stores in Sedgeford proudly announces the village's unique find. *Photograph by Terry Baxter*

6 Day two and the national media arrive to record frantic activity on site. Nine-year-old Harriet Mackie cleans finds with a toothbrush helped by SHARP supervisors Megan Dennis and Helen Thirkettle as the TV cameras roll. *Drawing by Harriet Mackie*

Tree roots were not the only problem that morning: the media had been invited. The hoard was publicised first to those local press, radio and TV outlets that had covered the project in the past. They quickly passed the story on to the nationals. By the end of the day, the Sedgeford hoard had been reported on BBC Radio Two and Four, on Yorkshire and Anglia TV, and even on Sky satellite global news (5 and 6).

Kev Woodward, SHARP volunteer:

> I was really looking forward to finding out more about the context in which the hoard had been buried. Unfortunately, the media had other ideas, and I spent the whole day being interviewed by different TV channels, radio and newspapers. By the end of the day I was thoroughly fed up with being asked to 'move just an inch to your left/right/up/down/in/out', etc.

Hilary Scase, Yorkshire Television *news reporter:*

> What I remember most clearly is the excitement when the gold coins were discovered. I was first told about them by Chris Mackie, and initially I thought he was putting a bit of a spin on the story to get some coverage. He convinced me, however, and I was soon out at Sedgeford to see for myself

and do an interview. Once there, I was infected: I could feel the excitement of everyone around me. I had never seen or been involved in anything quite like it before. Gold coins hidden in a cow bone. Unique. It is not a word I use lightly. But it is a word I used happily in this case. Were they really hidden in a time even before Boudica?

Duncan Hall, Lynn News *reporter:*

I was hunting around for a front-page lead story for the *Lynn News* when Chris Mackie called me. He simply invited me to a press conference the following day. Jokingly, I asked him if it was front-page material. I was quite surprised when he said 'yes' … The first thing I spotted when I got there was a photo of a number of gold coins – instant headline: 'Sedgeford strikes gold' – but then I heard the real mystery behind the find. A muddy cow's bone filled with 20 gold coins: was this some ancient version of a purse or an offering to ancient gods? … The hoard's finder was still on cloud nine, scarcely believing his discovery. And thanks to the way SHARP works, he was not just going to see it carted off to some museum or research lab on the other side of the country. He was going to be the one doing most of the investigating himself – digging the coins out of the mud inside the bone.

Sue Skinner, Eastern Daily Press *reporter:*

I was delighted to be there when the discovery of the gold hoard was announced on a glorious summer's day last August. Even better was watching Kev Woodward, who found the hoard, gently teasing the remainder out of the cow bone the following day.

A controversial decision had, in fact, been taken: the X-ray had shown there were no corrosion products inside the bone; the removal of the coins would therefore be a simple matter of careful extraction by hand (while creating a full written and photographic record): no specialist skills were required. In view of this, SHARP intended to follow its usual practice of granting its volunteers, with appropriate guidance and supervision, ownership of the entire archaeological process: in this case, that meant the finder of the hoard would also be its excavator.

THURSDAY 14 AUGUST 2003

Anj Cox, a SHARP director and professional archaeological illustrator, had spent much of the previous day drawing the bone as a precaution against it breaking up during excavation (*7*). Kev Woodward had, to his great surprise, been invited to prepare himself to excavate the coins.

Kev Woodward, SHARP volunteer:

> I left the campsite at 5.45am (I could not sleep properly) to drive to the 24-hour supermarket in King's Lynn. The shopping list included distilled water, a syringe or pipette and, if possible, long plastic tweezers. After breakfast, one of the human remains team gave me a bag crammed full of odd-shaped plastic and wooden tools. The bone excavation team then walked up to the Old Village Hall, SHARP's HQ, where the photographers were busy setting up their equipment.
>
> I chose the place I wanted to work and set up. The bone was supported in a bowl of sand covered by a plastic bag to retain the soil removed for archaeo-environmental analysis and protect the damp bone. All the tools were laid out and an overhead light complete with magnifier was put in position. The whole thing looked like an operating theatre, with me as the surgeon! (*8*)

7 Andrea (Anj) Cox retires to the relative calm of the Old Village Hall, SHARP's headquarters, to draw the hoard bone. *Photograph by Jim Reid*

8 SHARP volunteer Kev Woodward prepares himself for the operation ahead. Having found the hoard on site, in keeping with SHARP's democratic philosophy, Kev was asked to excavate the coins from inside the bone. *Photograph by Hilary Snelling*

The bone was photographed before excavation. A copy of the X-ray was projected onto a wall of the hall with an overhead projector and the visible coins were numbered. Each coin was to be tracked: a unique number and separate bagging would ensure that a record was kept of where each had been located within the bone.

Kev Woodward, SHARP volunteer:

> Many photos were taken before the first coin was removed. This one was fairly well wedged between another and the side of the bone, and took more pressure to release than I expected. Once out, and washed in distilled water, it was handed to the finds team. The second coin was now loose, and, after more recording and photos, it too was removed. We continued in this manner for the next six coins. Very little soil was now left in the bone, and the final cleaning out revealed a beautiful sight I hope never to forget: at least eight gold coins stacked one on top of the other and all shining back at me like they were made the day before (*colour plates 2-5*).

BBC Radio Norfolk news reporter Jill Bennett now arrived to do a live broadcast. Like so many others who came into contact with it over those few days, she was seduced by the allure of ancient gold.

Kev Woodward, SHARP volunteer:

> I let the radio reporter be the first person to touch one of the coins since its burial 2,000 years ago. She was speechless for about five seconds – on live radio – after I dropped the coin from the tweezers into her hand (9).

The excavation of the last coins – from the bottom of the shaft – presented a new technical problem and elicited further improvisation.

Kev Woodward, SHARP volunteer:

> I was now getting to the bottom of the bone and the tweezers were not long enough to reach. The high-tech solution was to tape on two wooden spatulas. These worked well enough, though working in such a small space and getting adequate light down the bone without obscuring the view of the coins was getting difficult. Finally, at about 5.30pm, the twentieth and final

9 BBC Radio Norfolk reporter Jill Bennett presents a broadcast during excavation of the bone. SHARP director Chris Mackie (left) provides commentary, while Kev Woodward examines a newly excavated coin. *Photograph by Hilary Snelling*

10 Day three: early morning excavation on the hoard site. SHARP supervisors Megan Dennis and Martin Hatton (sitting on baulk) help record as volunteers work furiously to excavate the hoard pit. *Photograph by Jim Reid*

coin was removed and recorded. As much soil as possible was washed out of the bone. All the soil removed was to be examined for seeds or pollen to add to the overall picture.

The excavation of the bone complete, the temporary lab in the Old Village Hall was dismantled. The excavation of the find-spot and the post-excavation analysis of the coins had, however, only just begun (*10*).

FRIDAY 15 AUGUST 2003

Gareth Davies, SHARP director:

Over the first two days after the find, I can honestly say I worked harder and longer than at any other time in my archaeological career. The final week of the 2003 season ended for me with the removal of the fill of an Iron Age gully underneath the hoard find-spot, and by that time I was pretty knackered.

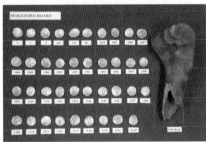
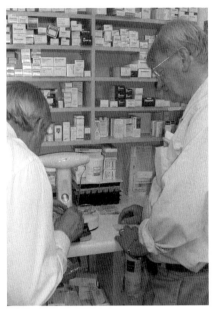

11 Above, left Recording the Sedgeford hoard. A glamorous publicity shot of the coins spilling from the bone (top). A more formal record shot of the complete hoard (bottom). *Photographs by Hilary Snelling*

12 Above, right A rural community rallies around its heritage. Local pharmacist Alan Stockley (left), surrounded by pills and potions, accurately weighs the gold coins, ably assisted by SHARP director Chris Mackie. *Photograph by Megan Dennis*

Young archaeologists, early in their careers, found themselves suddenly thrust under the spotlight of intense media and academic attention.

Megan Dennis, SHARP supervisor:

> It was a nerve-racking and exhilarating week. There was so much work to do. We were determined to prove our worth as a professional archaeological team, and to combine this with our commitment to education and community archaeology. There was the recording, drawing, photographing, scanning, cataloguing and weighing of the coins to complete, and all the paperwork associated with a treasure find to process (*11*).

SHARP is a community project in two senses. It offers local people an opportunity to see, help and, if they wish, participate in real archaeology.

But the community is also the base of resources and expertise that enables the project to function. The precise weighing of gold coins is an essential part of recording. Where do you go to get this done in rural Norfolk (*12*)?

Alan Stockley, Snettisham pharmacist:

At midday, midweek in August, my village pharmacy is usually quiet. The voice on the phone asked if I would be alone during the lunch hour. Intrigued, though a little wary, I said that I would, but, with an eye on the controlled drugs cabinet, I asked why. 'It's Chris [Mackie],' said the voice. 'We need someone with an accurate balance because of something we've found at the dig.' Just after 1pm, two shadowy figures knocked at the locked door. Chris and one of the archaeologists slipped inside – with a quick glance up and down the road.

Chris held up a collection of small polythene bags. 'Could you accurately weigh these?' He was hardly able to disguise his boyish excitement. One by one we decanted the coins and weighed them on the dispensary balance, recording the results and photographing the whole procedure. It was thrilling

13 Lining up for a look. Local residents gather at the excavation site to hear about how the hoard was found and for a chance to see 2,000-year-old Iron Age gold. *Photograph by Naomi Payne*

to be part of such an exciting episode, and I will always remember the experience of handling those little metal discs with their Celtic imprints, untouched by human hands for so many hundreds of years.

An important SHARP activity is the regular Friday afternoon site tour. The last of the 2003 summer season attracted record numbers (*13*).

Megan Dennis, SHARP supervisor:

> The highlight of the week for me was the site tour. After three or four days working from 7am to 11pm, stopping only for sandwiches, dinner and last orders at the pub, I was suddenly confronted by a marquee overflowing with expectant faces waiting for me to talk about the discovery. I managed to string a few sentences together, and then, while people queued patiently (in blistering heat) to catch a glimpse of the hoard inside a hastily-rigged display case, I tried to answer questions. It was seeing the enthusiasm and eagerness for information that fired us up to produce a book as soon as possible and share our knowledge with the people to whom the hoard really belongs: the local community.

Chris Mackie, SHARP director:

> Pat Chapman and I arranged the hoard in my display case, but we kept it covered with a cloth during the usual presentations by supervisors and volunteers about the week's work. Then Jim Reid [SHARP site technician] marshalled everyone outside the marquee and ushered them back in single file so that everyone had at least a brief look at the hoard. We felt we had done the right thing: everyone was so pleased and grateful for the chance to see the hoard so soon after discovery.

TUESDAY 16 DECEMBER 2003

After the season, because it was treasure, the hoard entered a legal process. It was passed to the British Museum, where it was officially recorded and reported on, and then became the subject of a local coroner's inquest back in Norfolk.

Tim Snelling, SHARP photographer (and local resident):

The coroner's inquest was held at 3pm on 16 December 2003 at St Margaret's House, King's Lynn. As well as the coroner (Bill Knowles) and his assistant (Michael Morgan), there were in attendance: three reporters from the press and radio; Kev Woodward, the SHARP volunteer who had found the hoard; Megan Dennis, the Iron Age supervisor; Chris Mackie, the publicity director; Hilary Snelling, another SHARP supervisor involved in recording the hoard; and myself.

Kev and Megan were the sworn-in parties (with odd informal interjections from Chris). The session lasted about 20-25 minutes, simply to verify that the hoard was found with the landowner's knowledge and consent, and that the find was more than 300 years old. It was mentioned that the hoard itself was still at the British Museum, but they did not want to retain it for their collection. Some idea of the current value of a Gallo-Belgic E gold stater [as the Sedgeford hoard coins were] was requested. A figure of about £200 was suggested.

In March 2004, the Treasure Valuation Committee met at the British Museum to decide how much the hoard was worth. The coins were valued at £7,500 (£192.31 each) and the bone container at £200. Though the British Museum did not wish to acquire the hoard, the King's Lynn Museum has now successfully raised funds to purchase it. After the refurbishment of the museum, due for completion in Spring 2006, the hoard will be displayed in the local community.

TWO

THE HOARD

INTRODUCTION

The Sedgeford hoard comprised at least 39 Gallo-Belgic E gold-alloy staters (large coins), dating to the early–middle first century BC (Haselgrove 1999). Twenty of these were recovered from inside the elbow end of a cow's front right humerus (upper leg bone). Eleven others were recovered from surrounding deposits and environmental samples during the summer 2003 season. Several others – almost certainly belonging to the hoard – had been found nearby in previous seasons: three in 1997, one in 1998, three in 2000 and one in 2001. The hoard, it seems, had been disturbed, the bone apparently broken and some coins scattered, perhaps in the Anglo-Saxon period when the site was used as a cemetery. Other coins may have been recovered at the time of this disturbance.

IRON AGE COINS IN BRITAIN

Coins first appeared in northern Europe in the late fourth century BC. These gold coins were produced in the reign of Philip II of Macedon (now northern Greece), and showed the wreathed head of Apollo on the front (the obverse) and a horse-drawn chariot and charioteer on the back (the reverse). They were used to pay the enormous armies of European mercenaries that Philip and his descendants used to build the Macedonian Empire. Many of these warriors returned home with their pay, and the locals began to produce their own coins based on the Macedonian models. Through

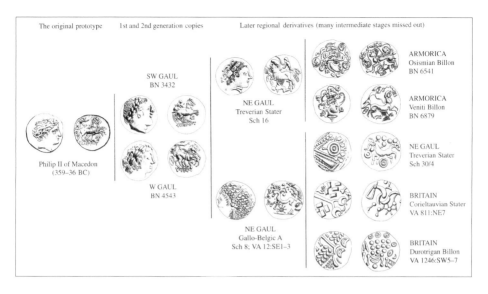

The original prototype   1st and 2nd generation copies   Later regional derivatives (many intermediate stages missed out)

SW GAUL
BN 3432

ARMORICA
Osismian Billon
BN 6541

ARMORICA
Veniti Billon
BN 6879

NE GAUL
Treverian Stater
Sch 16

Philip II of Macedon
(359–36 BC)

W GAUL
BN 4543

NE GAUL
Treverian Stater
Sch 30/4

BRITAIN
Corieltauvian Stater
VA 811:NE7

NE GAUL
Gallo-Belgic A
Sch 8; VA 12:SE1–3

BRITAIN
Durotrigan Billon
VA 1246:SW5–7

14 Chinese whispers. As coin-making spread across Europe, designs derived from Macedonian prototypes became more abstract. *Illustration courtesy of John Creighton*

continued copying, the designs soon became very different from the originals. Multiple horses were represented by a single horse, and chariots and charioteers became a stylised series of dots and symbols. Gradually, the use of coins spread across Europe (*14*).

By the beginning of the first century BC, coinage had reached Britain. The first coins in Britain were made from a copper alloy with high tin content called 'potin'. The prototypes of these coins were made in the Greek colony of Massalia (modern Marseilles in France), but the British ones were produced, and are commonly found, in Kent. Gold coins were imported, including an important series produced in northern Gaul (today northern France and Belgium) called 'Gallo-Belgic'. Like the original Macedonian staters, these imported coins were copied and local British variants began to appear. By the second half of the first century BC, coinages in gold, silver and copper alloy were being produced in different parts of Britain (*15*). During the first century AD, many became more 'Romanised', adopting classical styles and Latin inscriptions. Soon after the Roman invasion of Britain in AD 43, production ceased in Britain and coins were imported from Roman mints on the Continent.

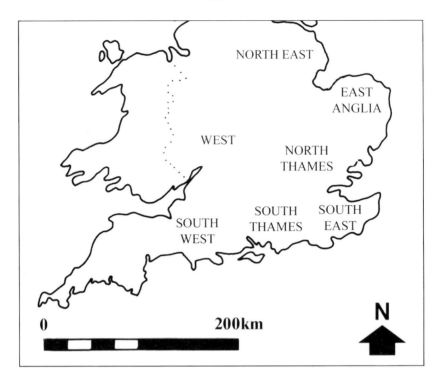

15 Where were coins made in Iron Age Britain? Coin specialists recognise that different types of coins were made in the areas shown above. Do these groups correspond with the Iron Age tribes referred to in historical sources – the Corieltauvi in the north-east, the Dobunni in the west, the Durotriges in the south-west, the Atrebates and Regni in the south Thames, the Cantiaci in the south-east, the Trinovantes and Catuvellauni in the north Thames and the gold-loving, torc-wearing Iceni in East Anglia? *Illustration by Andrea Cox*

GALLO-BELGIC E STATERS

The Gallo-Belgic series of coins from northern Gaul were perhaps minted by the Ambiani tribe (Allen 1980, 78). These coins were first studied in the 1960s by Derek Allen who arranged them into a series and devised the tra-ditional nomenclature (Gallo-Belgic A-F). The series began in the second quarter of the second century BC with a broad, flat gold coin based on the Macedonian stater. These depicted a head and a horse in wild and flamboy-ant style (Allen 1980, 20). They were the first gold coins to be imported in quantity into Britain, where they are known as Gallo-Belgic As. Later coins in the series, including Gallo-Belgic Es, were smaller and thicker, and the elements of the design became more abstract (*16*). Gallo-Belgic Es were struck in large numbers, having an output greater than any of the earlier types. They were issued in the early-middle first century BC, perhaps during the Gallic War of 58-51 BC (Scheers 1977, 343). They may have been used to pay men fighting Caesar's legions, and the Ambiani may have been minting coins on behalf of a wider confederation of anti-Roman tribes.

Gallo-Belgic Es all have the same design. The obverse, which would normally portray a head, is usually blank. Some examples, however, have the faint marks of worn-out designs with dots, lines and zigzags. Using blank or worn-out obverse dies must have facilitated mass production. The reverse is very similar to the Gallo-Belgic C design (and the earliest Gallo-Belgic Es were in fact struck using reverse dies from the minting of Gallo-Belgic Cs). The design shows a stylised horse facing right. The head is depicted as a triangle. The front legs are detached. In front of the horse is an oval ornament with a pellet (round dot) inside it. Above the horse are further small design elements, including a double pellet, a crescent, a torc, and a triple pellet. Behind is a 'spider' and a second oval and pellet. These features of the design are derived from the dismembered parts of the charioteer on Macedonian staters, but some, perhaps all, may have acquired new meanings along the way. The arms of the charioteer, for instance, seem to have been transformed into a Celtic torc. Beneath the horse is another crescent and pellet, and under the line beneath it (the 'exergual' line) appear various decorative border elements.

Not all Gallo-Belgic Es are the same. Weight, gold content and details of design vary, such that the coins can be arranged chronologically into seven

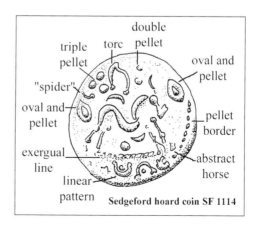

16 The anatomy of a Gallo-Belgic E stater. *Illustration by Ray Ludford*

main types (*17*) (Scheers 1977, 334). Probably, they were produced in such numbers that many dies wore out and had to be replaced (giving rise to subtle changes in design), and, in the face of prolonged military action, the gold content of coins may have been reduced as supplies of precious metal dried up (a change evident in the colour of the later coins and their slightly reduced weight).

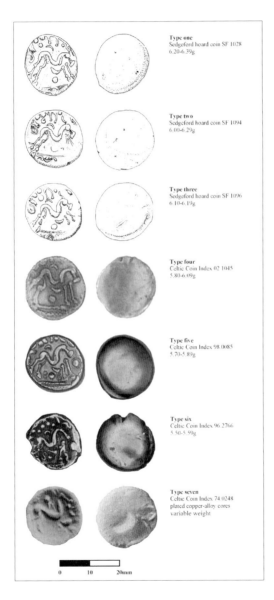

Type one
Sedgeford hoard coin SF 1028
6.20-6.39g

Type two
Sedgeford hoard coin SF 1094
6.00-6.29g

Type three
Sedgeford hoard coin SF 1096
6.10-6.19g

Type four
Celtic Coin Index 02 1045
5.80-6.09g

Type five
Celtic Coin Index 98 0085
5.70-5.89g

Type six
Celtic Coin Index 96 2766
5.50-5.59g

Type seven
Celtic Coin Index 74 0248
plated copper-alloy cores
variable weight

0   10   20mm

17 The seven types of Gallo–Belgic E stater. *Illustrations by Ray Ludford, photographs courtesy of the Celtic Coin Index*

All types of Gallo-Belgic E have been found in Britain except Type 7. Types 2 and 4 are the most common single finds and Types 1, 2 and 3 are the most common in hoards. Finds are concentrated in Kent and Essex, but the wider distribution stretches from Sussex to the Wash and East Yorkshire (*18*).

Soldiers returning home with their pay could have brought these – Caesar himself comments that 'in almost all the Gallic campaigns the Gauls received reinforcements from the Britons' (*The Gallic War*, V, 1) – though bulk payments to chieftains supplying men are also possible, especially in the case of large hoards. Other interpretations are that the coins were brought by refugees fleeing with their life savings; by invaders from northern France; or that they arrived through trade or gift-exchanges.

THE COMPOSITION OF THE SEDGEFORD HOARD

Though the Sedgeford hoard as recovered is composed of 39 Gallo-Belgic E gold staters, the original total is unknown and is likely to have been higher; the area where the coins were found is heavily disturbed. All the coins are of Types 1, 2 or 3, though several examples were hard to identify, the diagnostic linear pattern below the horse being absent from the design.

Comparison with other Gallo-Belgic E hoards from Britain reveals this to be a fairly typical hoard with no 'unusual suspects'. Most contain only Types 1, 2 and 3, with only a few unusual hoards also including Type 4s. The

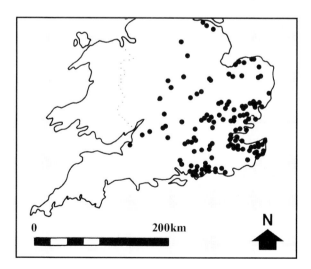

18 The find-spots of Gallo-Belgic E staters in Britain. *Illustration by Andrea Cox*

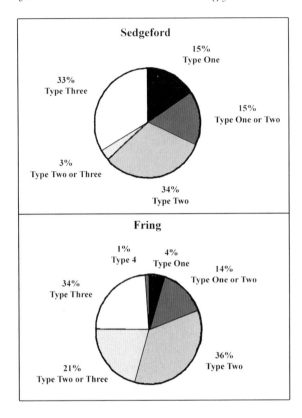

19 The composition of the Sedgeford and Fring Gallo-Belgic E hoards. *Illustration by Megan Dennis*

nearby Fring gold hoard, found only two miles from Sedgeford, contained 173 coins. Despite the much larger size of this nearest Gallo-Belgic E hoard neighbour, the composition of the Sedgeford and Fring hoards are broadly similar, though Fring has slightly fewer Type 1s and includes a single Type 4 coin (*19*).

DIE LINKS

A large number of reverse dies have been recorded for Gallo-Belgic Es (estimates suggest over 1,500 were used [de Jersey 1996, 18]). It is significant, therefore, that within the Sedgeford hoard several coins have been struck using the same reverse die. The die-links – which can be observed using the coin catalogue – are: coin 1112 with coin 1116, coin 3 with coin 1091, coin 451 with coin 1106, and coin 1087 with coin 1113.

1 'Pegasus' in his pit. This Iron Age horse, discovered on the same day as the hoard and named by those who excavated it, may have been ritually slaughtered and buried in a pit. *Photograph by Hilary Snelling*

2 'Two gold coins appeared.' Kev Woodward's first view of the Sedgeford hoard. *Photograph by Maria Fashing*

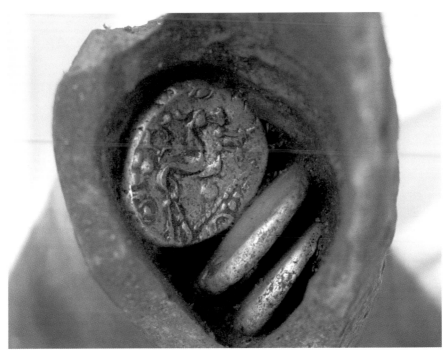

3 'A beautiful sight I hope never to forget.' The view down the bone shaft seen by Kev Woodward after excavation of the first two coins. *Photograph by Maria Fashing*

4 'Like they were made the day before.' Excavation continues down the stack of coins within the bone. *Photograph by Maria Fashing*

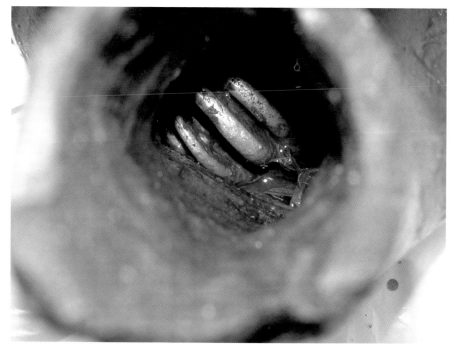

5 'Finally, at about 5.30pm, the twentieth and final coin was removed.' The last few coins to be excavated from the bone. *Photograph by Maria Fashing*

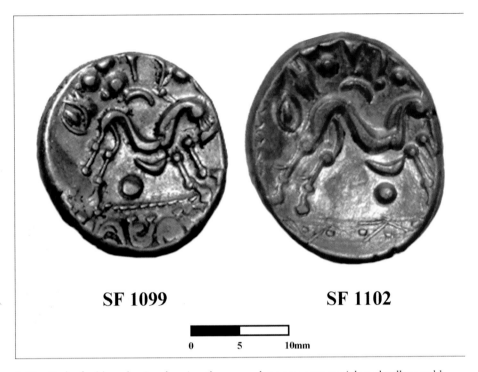

SF 1099   **SF 1102**

0   5   10mm

6 Two Sedgeford hoard coins showing the unusual orange copper-rich and yellow gold-rich areas on their faces. *Photograph by Maria Fashing*

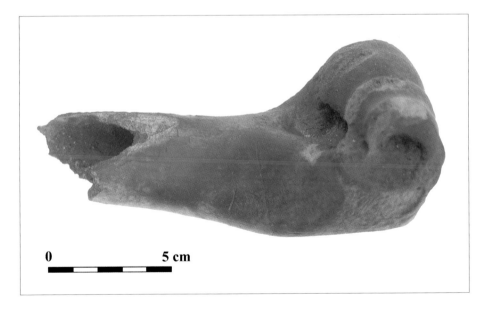

0   5 cm

7 The Sedgeford hoard bone – the broken lower part of the upper right front leg-bone of a cow. *Photograph by Maria Fashing*

8 View of the Boneyard–Reeddam site looking south over volunteers excavating the hoard find–spot. *Photograph by Jim Reid*

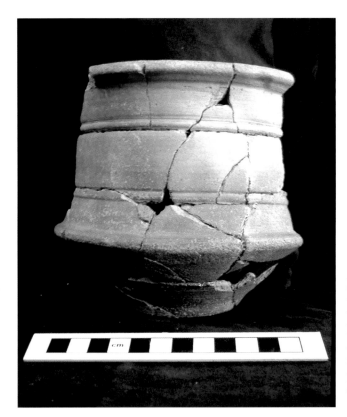

9 A Late Iron Age imitation 'Gallo-Belgic' vessel deposited at the base of a ditch, shown here after excavation and restoration. Could it have been deliberately placed as an offering to a deity? *Photograph by Terry Baxter*

10 The Sedgeford hoard. *Photograph by Hilary Snelling*

11 The Sedgeford torc fragment found in 1965. *Photograph © The British Museum*

12 The missing terminal from the Sedgeford torc. It was recovered in 2004 by SHARP almost 40 years after the original fragment was found. *Photograph by Hilary Snelling*

13 Gold Freckenham-type East Anglian Iron Age gold coin from Sedgeford found during fieldwalking in 2004. *Photograph by Chris Mackie*

14 Iron Age Sedgeford: bloodthirsty and warmongering? Did British mercenaries fight against Julius Caesar in Gaul for gold? *Photograph courtesy of the Museum of the Iron Age, Andover © Hampshire County Council Museums & Archives Service*

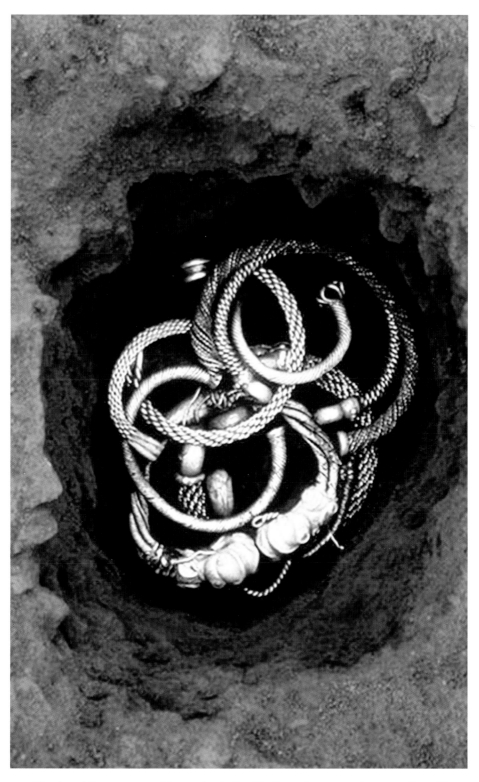

15 The Snettisham torcs – a fabulous haul of gold, silver, electrum and copper–alloy objects.
Photograph © The British Museum

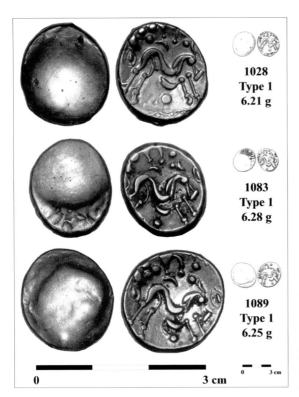

1028
Type 1
6.21 g

1083
Type 1
6.28 g

1089
Type 1
6.25 g

0   3 cm

Figs 16-28:
Catalogue of the hoard

16 Coins 1028, 1083 and 1089.
Note the clear straight zig-zag
on the exergual line of 1028.
Photographs by Hilary Snelling

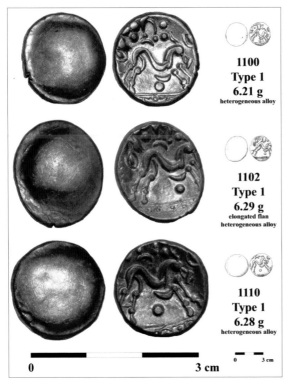

1100
Type 1
6.21 g
heterogeneous alloy

1102
Type 1
6.29 g
elongated flan
heterogeneous alloy

1110
Type 1
6.28 g
heterogeneous alloy

0   3 cm

17 Coins 1100, 1102 and 1110.
Colour differences are especially
clear on the obverse of 1102.
Photographs by Hilary Snelling

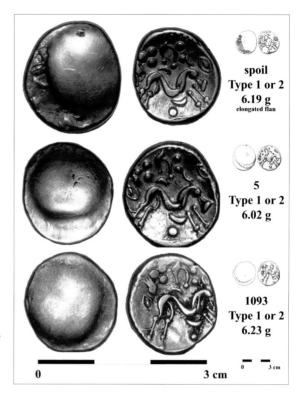

18 Coins spoil, 5 and 1093. Because the exergual line is missing from the bottom of these coins it is difficult to identify whether they are Type 1 or 2. *Photographs by Hilary Snelling*

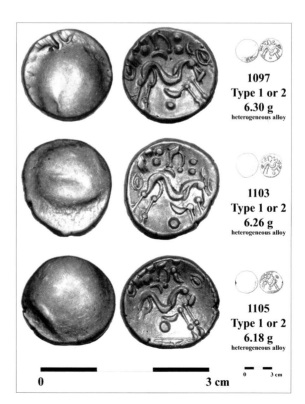

19 Coins 1097, 1103 and 1105. The markings on the reverse of coin 1097 are more typical of Type 1 coins. *Photographs by Hilary Snelling*

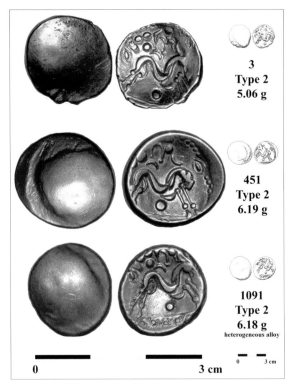

3
Type 2
5.06 g

451
Type 2
6.19 g

1091
Type 2
6.18 g
heterogeneous alloy

0   3 cm

20 Coins 3, 451, and 1091.
Coin 451 shows the far edge
of the design bordered by a
circle of pellets. *Photographs by
Hilary Snelling*

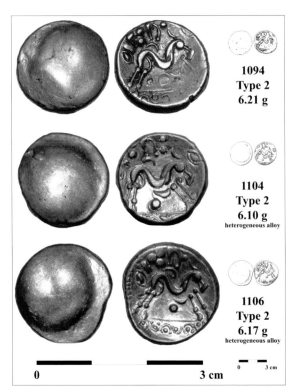

1094
Type 2
6.21 g

1104
Type 2
6.10 g
heterogeneous alloy

1106
Type 2
6.17 g
heterogeneous alloy

0   3 cm

21 Coins 1094, 1104 and
1106. Coin 1106 clearly shows
the crescents and pellets of
the exergual line typical of
Type 2 coins. *Photographs by
Hilary Snelling*

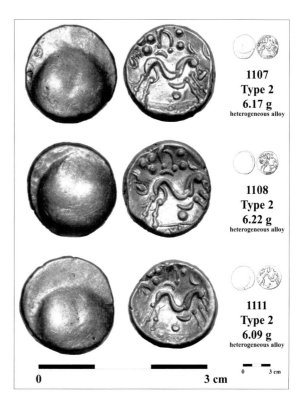

22 Coins 1107, 1108 and 1111. The flat parts of the reverses form when the coin is struck off-centre. *Photographs by Hilary Snelling*

1107
Type 2
6.17 g
heterogeneous alloy

1108
Type 2
6.22 g
heterogeneous alloy

1111
Type 2
6.09 g
heterogeneous alloy

0   3 cm

0   3 cm

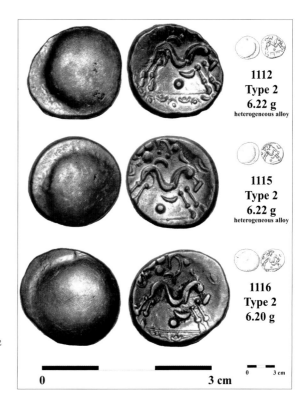

23 Coins 1112, 1115 and 1116. The horse of the obverse of 1112 is very tall with long legs – a typical Type 2 horse. *Photographs by Hilary Snelling*

1112
Type 2
6.22 g
heterogeneous alloy

1115
Type 2
6.22 g
heterogeneous alloy

1116
Type 2
6.20 g

0   3 cm

0   3 cm

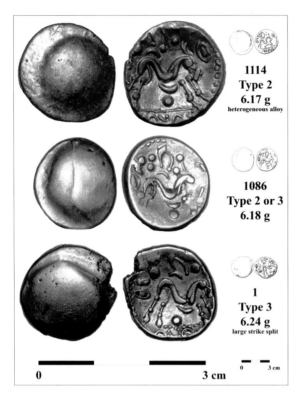

1114
Type 2
6.17 g
heterogeneous alloy

1086
Type 2 or 3
6.18 g

1
Type 3
6.24 g
large strike split

24 Coins 1114, 1086 and 1. There is a large strike split on coin 1 formed when the coin was struck. *Photographs by Hilary Snelling*

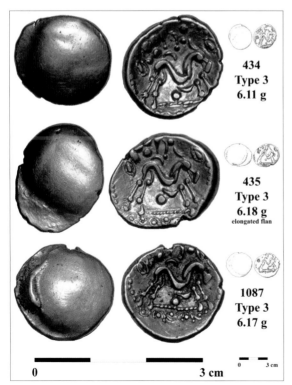

434
Type 3
6.11 g

435
Type 3
6.18 g
elongated flan

1087
Type 3
6.17 g

25 Coins 434, 435 and 1087. Coins 435 and 1087 show the pellet border on the left edge of the design. *Photographs by Hilary Snelling*

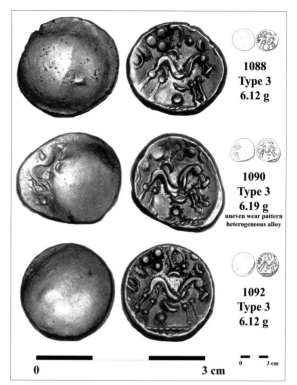

1088
Type 3
6.12 g

1090
Type 3
6.19 g
uneven wear pattern
heterogeneous alloy

1092
Type 3
6.12 g

0   3 cm

26 Coins 1088, 1090 and 1092. Coin 1090 was struck with a pair of clashed dies – they had been struck together with no blank between them resulting in the imprint of the obverse design on the reverse die. *Photographs by Hilary Snelling*

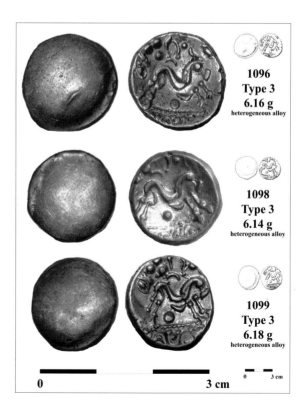

1096
Type 3
6.16 g
heterogeneous alloy

1098
Type 3
6.14 g
heterogeneous alloy

1099
Type 3
6.18 g
heterogeneous alloy

0   3 cm

27 Coins 1096, 1098 and 1099. The row of pellets making the exergual line of Type 3 coins is clearly seen on all 3 coins. *Photographs by Hilary Snelling*

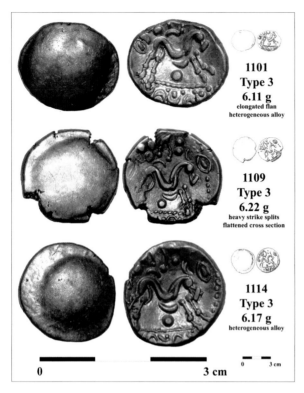

1101
Type 3
6.11 g
elongated flan
heterogeneous alloy

1109
Type 3
6.22 g
heavy strike splits
flattened cross section

1114
Type 3
6.17 g
heterogeneous alloy

0   3 cm

0   3 cm

28 Coins 1101, 1109 and 1114. The strike splits on 1109 were caused when the coin was struck. *Photographs by Hilary Snelling*

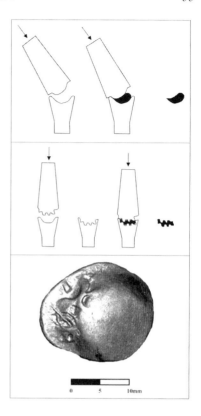

20 Poor quality control on a rushed job? Striking a coin with diagonal force produces an uneven coin (top). Dodgy dies – hitting the dies together without a blank between them impresses the reverse design onto the obverse die (middle). Coins struck later then have merged images (bottom). *Illustrations by Megan Dennis, photograph by Hilary Snelling*

Each die produces (at a conservative estimate) around 1,000 coins before breaking (de Jersey 1996, 18). Therefore, given the huge numbers of Gallo-Belgic Es produced, coins struck with the same die are likely to be found together only if they were kept together since being struck. This means that the four die links within the Sedgeford hoard may indicate that several smaller groups of coins, kept together since they were minted, had been united.

UNUSUAL COINS

Several of the coins (small finds (SF) numbers 3, 435, 1093) have been struck off-centre, resulting in an uneven shape. This occurred when the upper and lower dies were not properly aligned, for instance if the coin was struck with diagonal rather than vertical force (*20*).

Several coins (SF 1087, 1088, 1100, 1109) also have striking cracks (splits at the edges of the coin). Coin SF 1109 is very heavily cracked. This happened where the blank had not been heated sufficiently, or had been allowed to cool too much, before striking – a particular problem with alloyed gold, which is not as soft as the pure metal.

Some of the coins (SF spoil, 435, 1101, 1102) are not circular in shape. Close attention had not been paid when the coin blank was hammered into shape in preparation, resulting in an elongated rather than circular coin.

Among the coins from the hoard are two (SF 1090, 1102) possibly struck with clashed dies. If dies were accidentally struck without a blank between them, the blank obverse die would be faintly impressed with part of the design from the reverse. Coins struck subsequently using that die would have parts of the reverse design impressed onto their obverse in negative.

Die clashes are quite common among Gallo-Belgic Es: seven of the 52 in the British Museum collection show traces of the reverse design in negative on the obverse (Burnett and Cowell 1988, 5). The high proportion of die clashes in this type of coin occurred because they were produced rapidly with poor quality control. In fact, all the unusual features are blemishes more likely to occur when minting is hurried or the minters unskilled – strong circumstantial evidence to support a production date at the time of the Gallic War (Scheers 1977, 334).

Some coins (for example, SF 1114) have lines radiating from the centre of the design. These were impressed from the die and resulted from the hand-striking process, though the exact mechanism responsible for them is unknown. They are relatively common on Iron Age coins, especially those of gold alloy, and have been used in the past to distinguish between authentic hand-struck coins and modern pressure-casts. As dies became worn, the lines became more pronounced.

PRESERVATION

All the coins are well preserved, though some are of variable colour, orange in places, golden yellow elsewhere (*colour plate 6*). Most of the coins of patchy colour were recovered from inside the bone. The colour differences may have been caused by differences in the alloy content. Orange areas contain more copper, the yellow more gold, and, if the alloy components were not properly mixed when they melted, colour differences across a coin could result. Other Gallo-Belgic Es are homogenous in alloy content and colour, however, so the Sedgeford coins may have been affected after they were deposited.

It is possible that, within the enclosed, waterlogged environment of the bone, some leaching of the most mobile alloy component – copper – has taken place. Perhaps copper was removed from some areas of the coins, making these appear more golden yellow, and deposited over others, making them orange. Alternatively, the colour differences could have been caused by the deposition of iron on parts of the surface, or by some sort of interaction between metal and bone. Whatever the explanation, the phenomenon is unusual: the gold alloys of Iron Age coinage are generally stable and unlikely to undergo alteration under any archaeological conditions.

WEIGHT AND QUALITY OF PRECIOUS METAL

The weight (metrology) of the Sedgeford hoard coins broadly matches that of other examples both from the Continent and Britain. The Type 1s from Sedgeford may be slightly lower in average weight, but this may be due to increased wear relative to the 2s and 3s; the latter are of typical weight. This increased wear on Type 1 coins reflects the longer period they had been in circulation (chronologically they are earlier than Types 2 or 3), rather than any difference in the way they were used. One coin (SF 5) has an unusually low weight; this probably reflects lack of quality control during the generally rushed production of Gallo-Belgic Es.

The coins from the Sedgeford hoard have not been analysed for metallic content, but studies of other Gallo-Belgic Es shows them to contain around 60 per cent gold, 30 per cent silver and 10 per cent copper.

THE PLACEMENT OF THE COINS IN THE BONE

Detailed recording of the excavation of the cow bone revealed that the coins had been placed carefully and had moved minimally after deposition – despite the disturbance to deposits at the find-spot. The coins had been stacked horizontally in the shaft, though there had been slight disturbance at the base of the stack, where the hollow in the bone widens, and at the top, where coins had shifted position during later disturbance (*21*).

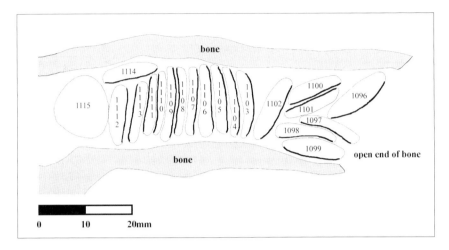

21 The orientation of the hoard coins in their bone container. The coins had been stacked horizontally but some had shifted since deposition. The thicker dark line indicates the reverse (horse) side of the coin. *Illustration by Megan Dennis*

DATING THE HOARD

None of the coins appears heavily worn, suggesting they were not in circulation long, an interpretation strengthened by the presence of die-linked coins within the group. The Type 1 coins are generally more worn than the 2s and 3s, but this is to be expected as they were produced earlier.

Dating the deposition of Gallo-Belgic E hoards is notoriously difficult. The coins are thought to have been minted in 58-51 BC in northern France – though some scholars would put it slightly earlier (Haselgrove 1999, 137; 1984, 84) – and there is little sign of wear on the coins forming the Sedgeford hoard. The uniformity of the hoard and the lack of later coin types, coupled with the presence of die links within the group, strengthens the likelihood of deposition soon after minting. It seems highly likely that the Sedgeford hoard was deposited soon after *c*.50 BC.

OTHER GALLO-BELGIC E HOARDS

Several other Gallo-Belgic E hoards have been found in Britain (*22*). They occur in a broad zone on the south-eastern side of the country. The Sedgeford hoard fits into this distribution, and is, in fact, the fifth Gallo-

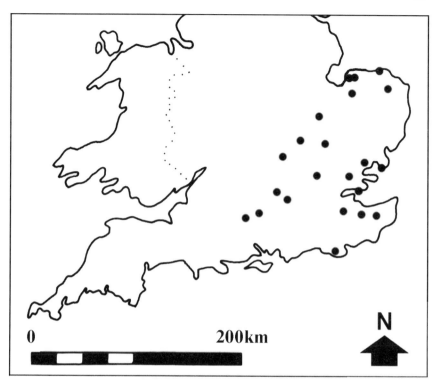

22 Gallo-Belgic E hoards found in Britain. *Illustration by Andrea Cox*

Belgic E hoard recovered from Norfolk (the others being Weybourne, with 39 coins; Fring, 173 coins; Buxton with Lammas, 14 coins; and Wormegay, seven coins). Four of these hoards are from north-west Norfolk, an area known generally for the richness of Iron Age finds and for a strong regional tradition reflected in characteristic types of monument, artefact and decoration (see chapter four). Two of the hoards were recovered in the Heacham valley (Sedgeford and Fring). The Fring hoard, recovered in March 1990, was significantly larger (at 173 coins) than that from Sedgeford. On the other hand, both hoards contained similar proportions of Types 1, 2 and 3 and the Sedgeford hoard may originally have been larger, perhaps much larger. Unfortunately, little is known about the Fring hoard: it has not been published, the coins have been sold and dispersed, and the find-spot has not been investigated.

It is now generally accepted that there is a broad scattering of Gallo-Belgic Es beyond the main distribution area of Kent and Essex. It is also assumed that Gallo-Belgic E hoards, which are distributed more evenly across the south-eastern zone, were all deposited shortly after the Gallic War – though there is no independent dating evidence, and it is always possible that the coins were kept for generations before deposition.

Why were the hoards buried? No general study has come to any firm conclusions. It is commonly assumed that the hoards were buried for safe-keeping by returning British mercenaries or Gallic refugees. 'Safety' burials, however, probably had a ritual dimension, and, where something is known, the local context of burial may support this: the hoards are probably not randomly distributed across the landscape, but occur at sites with sacred significance. The Fring and Sedgeford hoards were close by and of similar composition. Other rich Iron Age finds have also occurred in the area, notably the famous Snettisham torcs, but also including one gold torc from another part of Sedgeford itself. Are we seeing an extensive zone of ritual deposition in this area of north-west Norfolk?

ANOTHER HOARD IN A BONE

Only one other hoard dating to the Late Iron Age has been discovered hidden within a bone. It was found in 1893 by workmen in Honley, near Huddersfield, West Yorkshire (*23*) (Petch 1924). The bone (described as an 'ox bone') was 150mm long and much broken and decayed. It may origi-nally have been larger, but there was no record of associated bone fragments. The bone had been hidden in a small cavity within a rock. It contained a small bronze box with a decorated silver lid (perhaps a seal or perfume box); a bronze brooch dated to the first century AD; two small bronze rings (apparently miniature terret rings used to guide reins on horse-drawn vehi-cles); a total of 18 Roman coins, comprising 13 silver *denarii* dating up to the time of Nero (AD 54-68) and five bronze coins dating up to the time of Vespasian (AD 69-79); and five Iron Age coins from north-east Britain (three inscribed *VOLISIOS DUMNOVELLAUNUS*, one *VOLISIOS DUMNOCOVEROS*, and one *CARTIVEL*).

The Roman coins date this hoard to the last quarter of the first century AD, making it about a century later than that from Sedgeford. It should still, however, be regarded as essentially an Iron Age cultural phenomenon: this part of Britain was only conquered by the Romans in the AD 70s, and it always remained less Romanised than areas further south. Though the

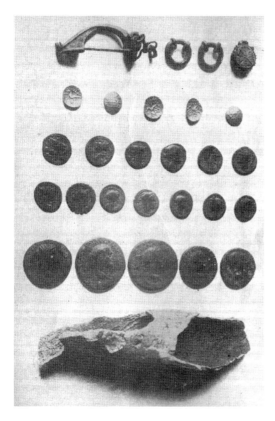

23 The Honley Hoard. Found in 1893 near Huddersfield, this is the only other Iron Age coin hoard found within a bone – but in this case dated 100 years later by the Roman objects also present. Sadly, the hoard was stolen from the Tolsen Museum in Huddersfield several years ago. This old photo is the only record of the find. *Photograph courtesy of the Tolsen Museum, Huddersfield*

practice was rare – only these two examples are known, and most contained hoards are recovered from within pottery – the hoard at Sedgeford is not a unique example of Iron Age coins contained within a bone.

CATALOGUE OF THE SEDGEFORD HOARD

The catalogue is arranged by Gallo-Belgic E types (*colour plates 16-28*). All the photos were taken by Hilary Snelling. Note that the photos were taken with a flash to increase the depth of focus and do not represent the true colour of the coins. In general the coins are more golden yellow than shown. The drawings are by Ray Ludford. Included in each catalogue entry is the SHARP small finds number, the weight of the coin in grams and, where necessary, additional notes.

THE BONE CONTAINER

The bone which contained the Sedgeford hoard is part of a right-hand-side cattle humerus (upper front leg bone) (*colour plate 7*) It consists of the distal epiphysis (elbow joint) plus about 30 per cent of the shaft. The lateral epicondyle (a part of the elbow joint) is missing. The bone shows no remarkable features and has the appearance of an ordinary bone from butchery or food waste. There is nothing to suggest that it had been specially selected for its purpose, nor any sign that it had been prepared or worked in any way.

The deep brown colour of the bone is characteristic of material recovered from the waterlogged area of the site. The shaft shows a clear chop-mark, the surface of which is slightly lighter in shade than the surrounding bone. It is arguable whether this has resulted from butchery before use as a hoard container, or is the result of disturbance of the site after deposition. It is not a fresh, modern break. The presence of a fragment of bone that may be derived from the hoard container – it has a similar thickness, but the fracture lines do not match – in the fill of the hoard pit indicates that the bone may have been broken in a later disturbance.

There are possible transverse cut-marks on the distal end of the shaft, but these lack the V-shaped profile to be expected from a knife score, and may thus have resulted from root erosion. Measurements of the bone show that it fits in comfortably with the known size ranges of Iron Age cattle.

The container, then, was an ordinary piece of bone. It would have been suitable for concealing valuables and, had it been unearthed by chance, would have increased the possibility of the coins remaining undetected (compared with, say, burial in a pot). On the other hand, the bone may have been selected because its ordinariness made it an effective representative of cattle/animal husbandry and the importance of food resources. Its ordinariness, in other words, does not preclude a ritual function.

To explore this possible ritual interpretation of the Sedgeford hoard further, we must broaden our view. Was it a security cache, a votive deposit, or both? To answer these questions, we need the wider context.

THREE

THE SITE

THE HOARD PIT

The hoard had been found during a routine metal-detecting scan prior to the end of the summer 2003 season on the Boneyard excavation site at Sedgeford (24). We had dug into the archaeology to remove the hoard bone, but once the importance of the discovery was clear, we chose to investigate the area thoroughly. Our aim was threefold: to reveal Iron Age features and recover other finds associated with the hoard; to understand the processes of later disturbance which had dispersed at least half the coins from the hoard; and to explore how the hoard fitted into a wider Iron Age context on the site (25).

We marked out for investigation a small area on the northern edge of Boneyard Field, where our 'Old Trench' (as opposed to the 'New') was separated by a narrow baulk from the waterlogged Reeddam Trench beyond (*colour plate 8*). Our volunteers dug all the deposits by hand in a series of small arbitrary spits (horizontal slices) and quadrants (vertical quarters). This method was intended to help us record the archaeology if the pit turned out to be complicated. All finds were kept, whether recovered during excavation or during wet-sieving of the spoil, and the position of all finds from the excavation was three-dimensionally recorded. All spoil was also metal-detected, and when the excavation was finished, a final scan was carried out over the whole area to check that all metal objects had been recovered. Written records, plans, section drawings and photos were made to ensure a thorough and accurate record. We can therefore describe the basic sequence of events in the place where the hoard was discovered.

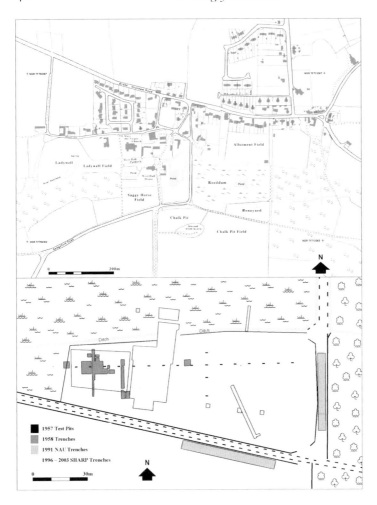

Before the hoard was buried, there was an Iron Age gully, 0.5m wide, running south–west to north–east through the area, which may be related to similar features found in the Reeddam Trench immediately to the north (*26*). The hoard bone had been placed in a circular pit (0.54m by 0.42m across) which cut into the fill of this gully. When the hoard bone was removed, Kev and Terry had dug only 0.24m into the south-eastern part of the pit. As well as the hoard bone, four more dispersed coins were found in this area, one of which was lying on the side of the pit cut. These four coins must have been detached from the hoard bone as the pit was filled, as there was no evidence of later disturbance in the fill of the pit. Four fragments of Iron Age pottery were also found in this fill.

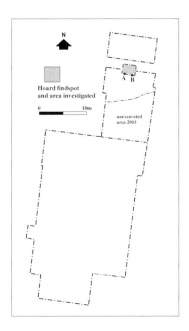

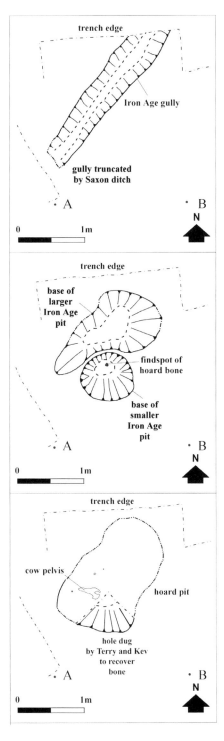

24 Opposite A map of Sedgeford village showing the various excavation trenches on the Boneyard-Reeddam site to the south. *Illustration by Andrea Cox, reproduced from Ordnance Survey based mapping on behalf of Her Majesty's Stationery Office © Crown Copyright 100043498 2004*

25 Above Plan of the Boneyard Old Trench and Reeddam Trench showing the hoard find-spot. *Illustration by Andrea Cox*

26 Right Gold in context – before, during and after the deposition of the hoard. First, an Iron Age gully (top). Then, a large pit, followed by a smaller pit containing the hoard (middle). Finally, the pits merged and filled up (bottom). *Illustration by Gareth Davies*

Next to the hoard pit was a second pit (1.55m by 0.9m), filled with similar material. We could not tell which pit had been cut first. The unusual
shape of the second pit, apparently truncated along its southern edge, might
imply that this was cut first, with the hoard pit cut into it. Both pits were
filled with a sandy light-grey deposit, similar to the natural sand around
them. There were small quantities of Iron Age pottery, oyster shell, animal
bone and human bone in the fill of the larger pit, but not such as to indicate
deliberate deposition (and some of this material, especially the human bone,
may have moved downwards through the soil from higher levels and thus
'intruded' into earlier deposits).

The pits had been deliberately backfilled with sandy earth in the Iron
Age. The remaining depressions had then been partly filled in with natu-
rally-deposited silt, obscuring the edges of the features and making them
appear as one. The half-filled double-pit was then gradually covered by
a dark sandy-silt which was deeper on the north-western side, perhaps
because this part of the pit had been open for longer. The dark silt contained Late Iron Age and Middle Saxon pottery, charcoal, and human bone
from at least one individual, the latter presumably originating from one of
the overlying Anglo-Saxon burials. At some point during the Middle Saxon
period, the silt may have been disturbed, though the area was also heavily
affected by modern root action.

The dark sandy-silt forming the upper fill of the pit contained small
animal bones, fragments of shell, and well-preserved charred plant remains.
These were recovered for examination by archaeo-environmental specialist Val Fryer. The plant remains included oats, barley and wheat, and some
of the wheat grains were of the elongated 'drop form' and may be examples of the spelt wheat common in the Iron Age. Wild plants included corn
cockle, brome, black bindweed and vetch. There was also a small fragment
of possible hazelnut shell. Small bones of fish, amphibians and mammals, as
well as fragments of marine shells, were also present. This material seems to
represent a low-density scatter of general refuse from an occupation site:
there is no evidence here for any burnt offering or other deliberate 'ritual'
deposits in the hoard pit. The same is true of most of the large bones recovered during excavation – sheep/goat, cow, horse and bird (possibly wood
pigeon). Material like this is typical of the fills of other Iron Age features
on the Boneyard site. On top of the pit fill, and almost directly overlying
the hoard bone, there was a complete cow pelvis (innominate bone), with
only a section of the pubis broken and missing. This was most unusual:

27 Did a cow pelvis mark the spot? Amongst root disturbance (centre left), an unbroken cow pelvis was found above the hoard bone. *Photograph by Terry Baxter*

such a bone would normally be chopped up during butchery (Crabtree 1989). If the dark silt forming the upper fill had accumulated in the Iron Age, could this large bone lying flat on the surface of the pit have marked the location of the hoard beneath, itself contained within a (smaller) cow bone? Could the fact that these were the only cow bones found in the pit be significant (*27*)?

The silted-up hoard pit had been cut into by many later features (*28*). These later features included: a medieval ditch; a Late Saxon burial layer (which contained one of the coins and some Iron Age pottery); an area of disturbance where a tree had grown through the hoard pit in the Late Saxon period or later; a charnel pit for the reburial of disturbed bones; a Middle–Late Saxon burial; a Middle Saxon pit or ditch; a Middle Saxon gully that may mark the edge of the cemetery (and which contained another loose coin); and another pit, post-dating the hoard pit, possibly Iron Age in date, and certainly pre-dating the Anglo-Saxon features. Clearly, the area had been intensively used and disturbed after the burial of the hoard.

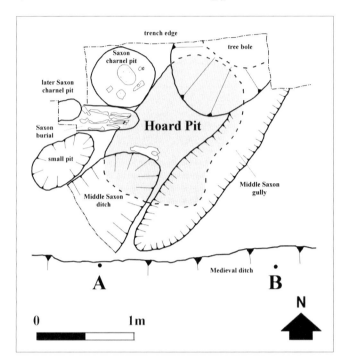

28 Hundreds of years later, when the hoard was forgotten, the pit in which it lay concealed was cut into by an Anglo-Saxon cemetery. *Illustration by Gareth Davies*

We can summarise the likely sequence of events as follows:

* An Iron Age gully was cut
* A large Iron Age pit was cut into this gully
* A small pit was cut into the southern edge of the large pit
* A cow's leg bone filled with 39 (or more) gold staters was placed in the small pit
* The small pit was then backfilled and the position of the hoard marked at the top by a complete cow's pelvis
* The large and small pits silted up and merged, and the cow's pelvis marking the spot was covered over
* Another (undated) pit was cut close to the hoard pit
* Middle Saxon burials, a charnel pit and a gully were cut into the hoard pit
* Tree roots grew into the hoard pit
* Late Saxon burials cut into the underlying deposits
* A medieval ditch was cut close to the hoard pit

If we conclude that the Sedgeford hoard was buried in a small pit and its position marked, this was a very deliberate act. What did it signify? To help answer this question, we looked at the other evidence for Iron Age activity on the Boneyard site.

THE IRON AGE SITE: A CONTEXT FOR THE SEDGEFORD HOARD

Boneyard Old Trench is still being excavated, but we have already identified several phases of Iron Age activity here and in the Reeddam Trench immediately to the north (*29*).

The densest concentration of Iron Age features (so far) lay beneath the Anglo-Saxon cemetery in Reeddam. Here we found several inter-cutting gullies. A large curvilinear gully (7046) contained a boar-tusk awl (for piercing holes in leather) and some 70 Iron Age potsherds. Of the latter, seven sherds

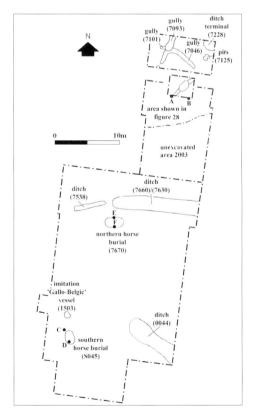

29 Plan of the Iron Age features excavated so far on the Boneyard-Reeddam site. The ground slopes steeply from south to north, and the hoard was deposited at the base of the slope (7662), possibly close to water. The area may have been marked out by large boundary ditches (7660/7630 and 0044) and associated horse burials (7670 and SO45). *Illustration by Gareth Davie*

could be joined together to form around 25 per cent of a complete vessel, and other sherds of the same distinctive, highly-friable fabric were also present. The remaining sherds were of small or medium size, and could therefore have been residual (that is, debris left over from earlier phases of activity).

The curvilinear gully, together with another east–west aligned gully (7101), was cut by a later, north–south aligned one (7093). The latter two gullies contained Iron Age pottery and worked, struck and burnt flint. Two postholes were excavated nearby, and two small inter-cutting pits (7125), containing Iron Age pottery, animal bone, flint flakes and a fragment of slag and crucible, were also found. The western pit contained one very large rim sherd and one medium-sized base sherd, which, with the addition of other, smaller sherds of the same high-quality fabric, appeared to form up to 15 per cent of a single vessel; again, there was a contrast with the rest of the potsherds, which had a residual appearance. The part-vessel was of 'Gallo-Belgic' type and probably dated to the first century AD.

In the north-eastern corner of the trench we found the terminal of a large east–west aligned ditch (7228), 1.7m in width, 0.4m deep, and containing five separate fills. The finds were notably different from those in the gullies, with little bone or pot (just ten small sherds) and even less flint. The lower fills appear to have slumped into the ditch from the northern side, possibly indicating the former presence there of an earth bank.

What does this evidence amount to? The gullies, postholes and pits may indicate a working enclosure with one or more associated round-houses; similar deposits interpreted thus have recently been excavated at Snettisham a few miles away (Flitcroft 2001). On the other hand, the monumental size of the large ditch terminal, the relative absence of occupation debris in its fills and the apparent deliberate deposition of part-vessels in gullies and pits – not to mention the hoard itself – may indicate ritual activity. Perhaps both interpretations are correct and the site changed use.

Other clues have been found in Old Trench. On the upper slope, in the southern part of the trench, part of a Late Iron Age imitation 'Gallo-Belgic' vessel was discovered in a heavily truncated feature (1503). The pot was the only artefact found, and it comprised about 35 per cent of a complete vessel, the 29 joining sherds arranged in such a way as to suggest that they had been broken *in situ*, either by a person or by the weight of the deposit above it (*colour plate 9*).

In the south-eastern part of the trench was an approximately 2m-wide ditch running north-west to south-east (0044). Presumably some sort of boundary, it appears to have been maintained for a long period, with up to 14 re-cuts in places. The upper fills contained substantial amounts of Middle Saxon pottery, but the earlier (undated) fills may have been Iron Age. Another large ditch, 2.5m wide and 1.2m deep, running east–west, was found on the lower slope (7660/7630), and this appears to have been aligned with a third, smaller ditch (0.7m by 0.25m) immediately to the west (7538). The pottery dating evidence includes an imitation 'Gallo-Belgic' sherd and a possible Roman sherd, implying that the ditches were in use until the Late Iron Age and only filled later.

Finally, there have been two horse burials. Neither has yet been radiocarbon dated, but stratigraphy and associated pottery clearly indicate an Iron Age date for one of them. The southern horse burial (S045) was truncated by later Anglo-Saxon burials, so that only the north–south oriented spine, ribs and legs remained (*30*). Though this burial is undated, its similarity to the northern horse burial makes it highly likely that it was contemporary.

The northern horse burial – found, coincidentally, on the very same day as the hoard – was nearly complete (*31* and *colour plate 1*). The horse was buried tightly packed into a pit measuring 1m by 1.8m across and around 0.5m deep. The legs were in a near-vertical position on the southern edge of the cut, the spine lay east–west and the head had been turned backwards into a 'looking over the shoulder' position, facing the terminal of the large east–west ditch (7660/7630) nearby. A single small sherd of Late Iron Age pottery was found in the pit fill, and the layer sealing the pit also contained Iron Age pottery, giving the northern horse burial a fairly secure date.

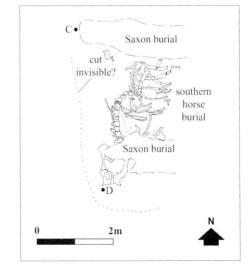

30 The southern horse burial as excavated. It was oriented with the head to the north and the hind legs to the south, but these parts of the skeleton had been cut away by later Anglo-Saxon burials. *Illustration by Gareth Davies*

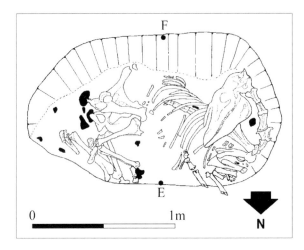

31 'Pegasus'. The
northern horse burial
as excavated. In this
case, the burial was
found complete, but was
orientated east–west.
Was the damage to his
forehead done during
a ritual sacrifice?
*Illustration by
Gareth Davies*

Evaluation trenches in other parts of Reeddam and Boneyard have also
revealed Iron Age evidence. About 15 per cent of an imitation 'Gallo-Belgic'
pot was found in part of a small gully excavated in 1996 in a test-pit about
20m east of the main Reeddam excavation. Another large Anglo-Saxon
ditch, 2.5m across, 1.6m deep and with evidence for at least eight re-cuts,
was found in an evaluation trench about 30m east Old Trench. This, like the
big ditch on the upper slope (0044), may have had an Iron Age origin, since
the earlier V-shaped re-cuts produced no pottery evidence, unlike the later
U-shaped ones which yielded Middle Saxon material.

There are two ways of looking at this evidence. A functional interpretation
would stress the way in which the three monumental ditches – in Reeddam
(7228), on the lower slope (7660/7630) and on the upper slope (0044) – may
divide up land according to different uses: for instance, valley floor, occupation area, working area and cultivated land. A ritual interpretation would stress
the monumentality of the ditches (and possible banks) and the character and
location of certain deposits: we might imagine the horse burials to be 'guard-
ing' the multiple entrances of a sacred enclosure, broken ceramic containers
to have been reverentially discarded – and, of course, the hoard of gold to
represent a rich offering to some unknown Iron Age deity. Or perhaps it was
first an occupation site and only later a ritual one? Or perhaps it was both at
once, north-west Norfolk in the Late Iron Age being a place when the real
and the spiritual were inextricably intertwined.

To find out, we need to review the comparative evidence from outside
Sedgeford.

THE TAPHONOMY OF THE HOARD

Taphonomy is the study of the processes that form archaeological deposits. Medieval, Anglo-Saxon and Iron Age features truncated the hoard pit. These truncations caused at least seven coins to be dispersed from the pit. Three further coins were located during metal-detecting of spoil, and these too had been dispersed beyond the hoard pit, since they were discovered before the latter's excavation. Another nine coins were found dispersed within the pit fill.

The excavation of the hoard pit was therefore a rare opportunity to observe the degree to which coins might be moved from a fixed point (the hoard bone) by later activity. Below is a schematic representation of the coins dispersed from the bone. The line running from hoard bone to coin find indicates how far each coin had moved.

It is impossible to know how many separate truncation events each coin had passed through. It is impossible to trace the movements of each coin through the full series of ditch re-cutting, animal burrowing and tree growth. There does, however, seem to be some patterning in the distribution of coins dispersed from the hoard (*32*).

The most likely candidate for the truncation event that dispersed most of the coins is a north-east to south-west aligned Anglo-Saxon gully which may have formed an early cemetery boundary. If this cut clipped the bone so that it was left lying horizontally (as found), it is likely that some coins would have strayed into the fill of the hoard pit (where seven were found) and that others would have been dispersed beyond it.

There is a definite cluster of dispersed coins that were located during the excavation of the Reeddam Trench. Coins SF 2, 5, 451 and 1028 may well have been moved away from the hoard pit during an Anglo-Saxon ditch-digging event. Perhaps these coins were moved north of the hoard pit when material from the ditch was used to level the ground for use as a cemetery. Alternatively, an unseen Iron Age or Anglo-Saxon cutting event may have dispersed the coins to the south, before later medieval ditch-digging threw them to their final, northern resting place. This, however, seems the less likely hypothesis, since no evidence has been found of a medieval bank north of the ditch, and anyway the dispersed coins were all found at a level lower than we would expect a medieval land-surface to be: coin SF 451 only 40mm higher than the top of the hoard pit-fill and at the very base of the Anglo-Saxon burial layer; coin SF 1028 only 90mm higher.

Coin SF 1 is the furthest dispersed coin and was found in the topsoil. Perhaps grave digging further dispersed this coin from the cluster formed by coins SF 2, 5, 451 and 1028. Coin SF 1089, on the other hand, may have been dispersed by tree-root action alone.

There are certainly limitations to these observations. We cannot be certain which cutting events were responsible for dispersing which coins. We cannot know what proportion of the original total of coins deposited in the hoard may have been removed from the site before our excavation. On the other hand, since the whole of Reeddam has been carefully excavated by hand, with systematic metal-detecting and wet-sieving, we can be confident that we have recovered all the remaining coins and that the pattern of dispersal recorded is a genuine one.

Millet has suggested that the analysis of surface artefact scatters located by fieldwalking could be made more productive by correlating these patterns with evidence recovered in excavation (1985). Slowikowski has further suggested that potsherds from the same pot dispersed through the ploughsoil could, especially if related to the truncated feature from which the pot originated, be used to measure artefact movement caused by post-depositional disturbance (1995). The dispersed coins from the Sedgeford hoard constitute, in this context, an especially useful case-study.

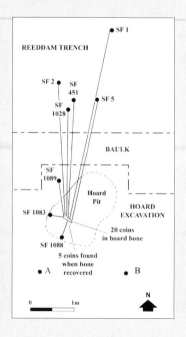

32 Twenty coins were found inside the hoard bone, but at least 19 more had been scattered by later activity. This diagram shows how far each of the dispersed coins had been moved. How far can the events causing this dispersal be reconstructed from the evidence? *Illustration by Gareth Davies*

FOUR

THE IRON AGE BACKGROUND

How does the Sedgeford hoard fit into the wider context of Iron Age Norfolk? SHARP's work on Iron Age settlement in the area began in 2000 AD, and our work has so far involved desktop research, field survey and small-scale excavation. The results allow us to picture Sedgeford in the first century BC, when the hoard was deposited. We are beginning to see where people lived, the types of objects they used, and the links they had with communities further afield. Theories are developing which interpret Sedgeford as part of a north-west Norfolk regional group that used similar objects and may have had similar beliefs and rituals.

PROBLEMS OF INTERPRETATION

Understanding the Iron Age of Sedgeford and north-west Norfolk is not easy. Lack of research in the area overall has led to the emergence of 'hotspots' of archaeological activity, such as the famous 'Gold Field' in Snettisham, where intensive excavation last century revealed at least nine hoards of gold and silver torcs, in contrast with other areas left unexplored. There is no evidence, for example, from the parish of Docking to the east of Sedgeford. Perhaps severe exploitation during the Neolithic exhausted the soils there and left them unable to support later communities (Robinson and Gregory 1987, 7), or it may simply be that so little archaeological research has been carried out in the parish that no evidence has been found.

The riches of north-west Norfolk are well known to metal-detectorists. Most record their finds, make accurate identifications and work in tandem with the archaeological authorities to ensure discoveries and find-spots are recorded. Unfortunately, criminals use metal detectors to make money, and looting of sites is rife in the region. The theft of 6,000 Iron Age coins and a silver vessel from the Gold Field is one example (Stead 1998). More often we simply do not know what has been taken. These losses greatly reduce archaeological knowledge.

In the Iron Age, of course, the village and parish of Sedgeford did not exist. We do not know where everyone was living or the name they used to refer to the area. For convenience, we use modern names – like Boneyard Field, Sedgeford, north-west Norfolk and East Anglia – but these are terms and divisions which did not exist in the Iron Age. The way in which pre-historic people thought about the landscape they inhabited was probably very different – and different, moreover, in ways we can only begin to imagine.

Until recently, East Anglia was something of a backwater in Iron Age studies (Hill 1999, 185), However, thanks to new excavations and pottery analysis (Percival 1999), studies of coinage (Chadburn 1990; Talbot forthcoming), and research based on the distribution of recorded finds (Hutcheson 2004; Dennis forthcoming), we are beginning to learn much more about Iron Age Norfolk.

SEDGEFORD

In the Iron Age, the valley that contains the village of Sedgeford looked different. Boneyard Field was drier. The river took a different route across the valley floor and it may have been navigable. Small boats or flat-bottomed punts may have travelled up and down, perhaps as far as Fring, the parish to the south-east, where a small pool in the river is known locally as 'the harbour'. Somewhere in the valley, the long stretch of connected tracks that linked this part of Norfolk to southern Britain (now known as 'the Icknield Way') crossed the river. The crossing would not necessarily have been formalised, and fording would have taken place wherever the water level permitted. The tracks generally followed the contours of the chalk ridge which runs roughly north–south through north-west Norfolk, placing them in the western part of the modern parish.

The undulating landscape on either side of the river was managed and exploited in this period. By the Early Iron Age (700–500 BC), no natural woodland remained. It had all been cleared to make way for agriculture and settlement during the Bronze Age (*c.*2000–700 BC), and had been managed for several centuries (Davies 1999, 18). The diversity of artefacts and food remains found in the Iron Age archaeological features on Boneyard indicate that this may have been the site – amongst other things – of a small farming settlement. People here seem to have grown cereals (spelt wheat, barley, oats), to have raised animals (sheep/goats, cattle, pigs, horses) and to have fished in the river. The additional discovery of slag and a crucible fragment implies that they also worked metals, as well as making domestic pottery using tools of worked flint and boar tusk.

Crops may have been grown in long, narrow 'co-axial' fields, fragmentary evidence for which has been detected fossilised in later medieval field-systems across East Anglia. The most famous example is south Norfolk's Scole-Dickleburgh field system, where the north–south alignment of the fields is bisected by the north-east/south-west line of the Roman Pye Road, which shows that the field boundaries must have predated the road (Williamson 1987, 1998, 2003; Hinton 1997). Other examples have been recorded at Yaxley, Suffolk (Williamson 1987); the Creakes, north-west Norfolk (Hesse 1992); south-east Cambridgeshire (Harrison 2002); west Cambridgeshire (Oosthuizen 1998, 2003); and throughout Hertfordshire (Williamson 2000). Similar patterns appear on the pre-enclosure maps of Snettisham, Heacham and Sedgeford itself; some of the latter appear to pre-date the Roman Peddar's Way, which, like the Icknield Way, passed through the parish (Williamson 2003).

Though we cannot be sure where people lived in the valley when the hoard was deposited, we know of several possible locations. From antiquarian investigations, modern excavations, and recent fieldwalking surveys we can identify a number of possible or certain Iron Age sites:

Sedgeford Hall
Early twentieth-century excavations revealed a large amount of Late Iron Age and Romano-British pottery (Ingleby 1925).

Polar Breck
Fieldwalking by SHARP in 2000 and 2004 recovered a scatter of Early Iron Age pottery in this field.

'Saggy Horse Field'
Excavations in the eastern portion of West Hall Long Meadow revealed two
Iron Age ditches and related postholes in 2003.

Boneyard/Reeddam
As well as the hoard itself, extensive evidence for ditches, pits and other
features has been excavated since 1997.

These sites have yielded a variety of pottery types. Crude, often fragile,
handmade wares were probably used for cooking and storage. In contrast, on
the Boneyard-Reeddam excavations, we have found examples of far more
robust, high-status, wheel-thrown pottery in a 'Gallo-Belgic' style, imitating
vessels produced on the Continent in the Late Iron Age. Were people living on the site when this pottery was in use? It is rare in Norfolk generally
(Percival 1999, 182), but it has been found on other sites in the north-west
of the county (Flitcroft 2001; Lewton-Braine 1953; Percival 1995). Other
high-status items have also been found in Sedgeford (*33* and *34*):

The hoard
39 Gallo-Belgic E staters contained within a cow bone were excavated
in 2003. (*colour plate 10*)

The Sedgeford torc
Two pieces of electrum (gold alloyed with silver) torc or neck ring with
similar decoration to the Snettisham torcs were recovered in 1965 and 2004
(*colour plates 11* and *12*).

33 The
Sedgeford
torc. This
fragment
was found
in 1965.
*Photograph
courtesy of the
Eastern Daily
Press*

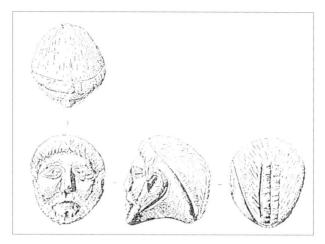

34 An Iron Age miniature head from Sedgeford – perhaps the end of a sword pommel? *Illustration from Norfolk Historic Environment Record 23321 drawn by Sue White copyright Norfolk Museums & Archaeology Service*

Terret rings

Two terret rings have been recovered in the parish. One was decorated with red enamel inlay. Terret rings were used to guide the driving reins on a horse-drawn chariot.

Copper alloy head

This 'Greek'-style head recovered by a metal-detectorist in the west of the parish may once have been used as a sword pommel.

Silver coins

One normal face/horse East Anglian coin was excavated in 2003 and a probable silver plated unit was found during field survey in 2004; both date to the first century BC or AD.

Gold coins

One early Freckenham-type East Anglian gold coin was recovered during field survey in 2004 (*colour plate 13*).

Sedgeford's Iron Age people seem to have been using metal objects which are unusual when compared with other East Anglian assemblages. The metal finds normally to be expected on Iron Age occupation sites, such as copper-alloy brooches or pins, have not been found. Instead, precious metal objects and copper-alloy horse fittings are more common than in the rest of East Anglia and Britain as a whole.

All these items were probably made locally, forming part of a distinctive regional assemblage in north-west Norfolk, though the models on which they were based lay further afield. It seems that Iron Age Sedgeford was not isolated. Its people shared a material culture and, most likely, a social structure, belief systems and ritual practices with the people of north-west Norfolk as a whole and, to some degree, with people beyond.

NORTH-WEST NORFOLK

The geography of the north-west region of the county in the Iron Age included the flat plain of the erratically drained marshes around The Wash and the higher, more undulating landscape formed by chalk and greensand outcrops to the east. River systems, including that which passed through the Sedgeford valley, emptied into The Wash at the interface between the chalk plateau and flatter clay-lands to the west. The region was bounded by the North Sea to the north, the elevated clay-lands of central Norfolk to the east, sandy heathlands to the south and by The Wash and the Fens to the west. It therefore developed its own characteristic site types and artefact assemblages during the Iron Age.

As already seen in Sedgeford, the evidence of field boundaries indicates clearance of woodland and a cultivated landscape throughout the area (Williamson 2003). Spelt wheat has been found in archaeo-environmental samples from excavations both in Sedgeford and on the Snettisham bypass (Flitcroft 2001, 79–80). Frequent finds of horse harness (including the Sedgeford terrets) show that there were horses throughout the area (35) (Hutcheson 2001).

Other animals were also managed, though they may be less archaeologically visible: bone assemblages show that people throughout the region had a similar diet to those living in Sedgeford; and the bones of a small pig and some Iron Age pottery discovered in a pit in Heacham (Lewton-Braine 1953) demonstrate that the Sedgeford horse burials were not unique deposits of whole animals.

Although sites are often difficult to identify in north-west Norfolk – mainly because they usually lack substantial archaeological features – the limited evidence available fits with that at Sedgeford. The ditches, gullies and pits excavated on Boneyard-Reeddam and the ditches and postholes found in 'Saggy Horse Field' correspond with the evidence from other Iron Age

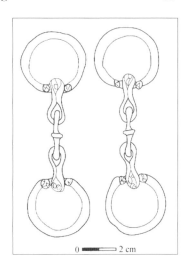

35 A horsy aristocracy? This pair of Iron Age copper-alloy bridle bits was found just beyond the northern edge of Sedgeford in the neighbouring parish of Ringstead. *Illustration courtesy of Natasha Hutcheson, based on photograph by R.R. Clarke*

0 ⟼ 2 cm

domestic sites in north-west Norfolk (Flitcroft 2001; Lewton-Braine 1953; Hill 1999, 190; Norfolk HER 13032). Typically, such sites were unenclosed.

Aerial reconnaissance has, however, identified two classes of enclosed site peculiar to north-west Norfolk: medium-sized enclosures and rectangular enclosures. The former have, in terms of function, been compared to the hill forts of southern England (Davies 1999, 30). They vary in construction, layout and location, but are found only in north-west Norfolk and often overlook rivers or the sea. Though one example has been identified at nearby Snettisham (Stead 1995), there does not appear to be one in the Sedgeford valley – though several crop marks have yet to be investigated and dated.

The other class of monument, the rectangular enclosures, are similar to Continental *viereckschanzen* (Iron Age enclosures characterised by a square or roughly square boundary enclosing an area of less than one hectare and with a single entrance; Davies 1999, 32). These monuments may have had a ritual role. The most southern example, excavated at Fison's Way, Thetford, incorporated funerary, domestic, industrial and ritual areas (Gregory 1991). Is a complex crop-mark in the Sedgeford valley, seen on an aerial photograph, a newly-discovered example of one of these structures (*36*)? In size, shape and siting it looks possible, but crop marks can rarely be reliably dated without further investigation. If this enclosure turns out to be Iron Age, then it may have been a centre for ritual practices and votive deposits by the people living in the valley and perhaps the wider region, or a meeting place, a defence-work, or, perhaps more likely, some combination of these.

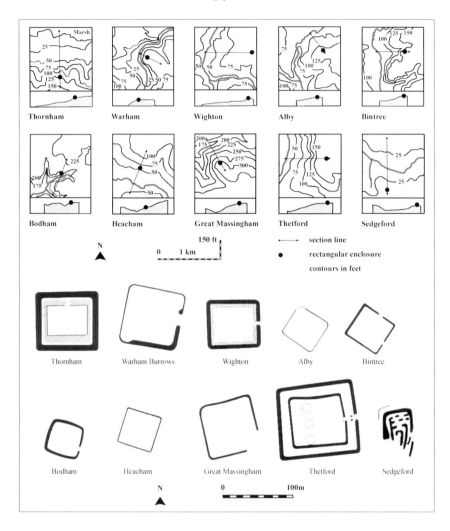

36 The position and layout of the Sedgeford crop mark in comparison with other similar sites in north-west Norfolk. The small maps show the locations of these sites, with cross sections through the landscape beneath (top). All are positioned overlooking marshes or river valleys. The site plans show that all have a rectangular layout, although they vary in size (bottom). Could the Sedgeford example be one of these Iron Age rectangular enclosures? *Illustration by Megan Dennis based on Gregory, T., 1986, 'Enclosures of 'Thornham' type in Norfolk', figs 26-7, in Gregory, T. and Gurney, D., 'Excavations at Thornham, Warham, Wighton and Caistor St. Edmund, Norfolk', East* Anglian Archaeology *30*

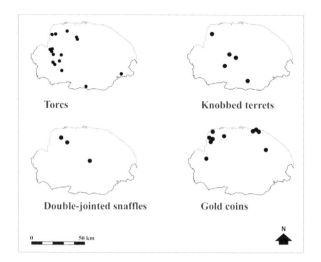

37 The distributions
of high-status metal
objects characteristic
of north-west Norfolk.
The Sedgeford hoard
is one example of
these characteristic
objects. *Illustration
by Andrea Cox from
original by John Davies*

The mixture of handmade and wheel-thrown pottery identified at Sedgeford is similar to those excavated at other sites in north-west Norfolk (Flitcroft 2001; Lewton-Braine 1953; Percival 1995). This region is the only part of the county where imitation Continental types were used (Percival 1999, 182; Lyons 1996). Locally made, high-quality metal objects are also characteristic of the region as a whole (*37*): there is a concentration of torcs, knobbed terrets and double-jointed snaffles (a type of bridle bit) in north-west Norfolk, as well as both imported and indigenous gold coins (especially hoards) (Davies 1996, 1999; Palk 1984, 62). Many of these objects are decorated in similar local styles (Clarke 1954, 65). So the Sedgeford assemblage is not unusual. And the Sedgeford hoard itself also fits into a pattern of Gallo-Belgic E hoards in north-west Norfolk as a whole.

The way in which rich metal objects were deposited also appears to be similar across the region (Hutcheson 2003, 94; Fitzpatrick 1992, 397). Where evidence is available, it suggests these objects were grouped together and then put into the ground in specially dug pits (*38* and *39*):

The Snettisham hoards of torcs and other objects
The Snettisham torcs – a fabulous haul of gold, silver, electrum and copper-alloy objects, many elaborately worked and decorated in the La Tène style – were professionally excavated during the twentieth century (Stead 1991) (*colour plate 15*).

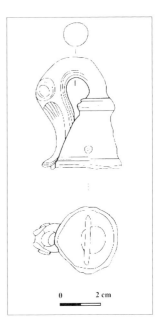

38 Above Gold hoard of Norfolk 'wolf' staters
found in Heacham. *Photograph courtesy of John Davies*

39 Right Drinking horn fitting from Snettisham.
Norfolk Historic Environment Record 25249 drawn by
Sue White, copyright Norfolk Museums & Archaeology
Service

0   2 cm

The Sedgeford torc
See above, page 56.

The Fring gold hoard
173 Gallo-Belgic E gold staters were recovered by a metal-detectorist from
a site near Fring.

The Heacham hoard
14 British J gold staters were metal detected from a small site near the mouth
of the Heacham river (Davies 1996, 72).

The Fring silver hoard
169 silver coins contained in an imitation Gallo-Belgic-style pot, covered
with a textile lid (Chadburn 1990; Chadburn and Gurney 1991), were excavated from a second site near modern Fring.

The Snettisham terret and drinking-horn
A copper-alloy and enamelled terret and a drinking-horn attachment were
found at sites close to the Snettisham torc hoards (Hutcheson 2003, 91).

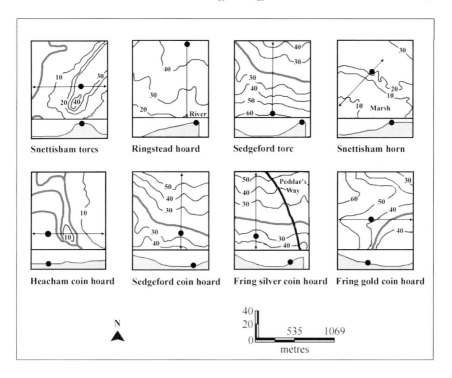

40 Torcs on the hill; coins in the valley: is this a pattern? The small maps show the find-spots of Iron Age object hoards (top) and Iron Age coin hoards (bottom) in north-west Norfolk. Cross sections through the landscape are shown beneath the maps. *Illustration by Megan Dennis*

The Ringstead horse-fitting hoard

Two copper-alloy bridle bits, two plates and rivets, a clasp, a strap union (a piece of horse harness), a cake or ingot of copper alloy and some fragments of metalworking debris were recorded in the 1950s (Clarke 1951, 514-525).

These rich objects were buried in one of two patterns in the landscape (*40*). Some items were buried in relatively high, isolated areas overlooking rivers – the Snettisham torcs, the Ringstead hoard and the Snettisham decorative drinking-horn and terret conform to this pattern. Alternatively, we see the burial of rich objects close to rivers near or on the valley floor – for example the Heacham, Fring and Sedgeford hoards. Because these objects are of similar types, were buried in a similar way and form patterns in their landscape contexts, can we suggest different reasons for their deposition? Could the rich objects buried in isolated, elevated positions represent ritual gifts to the gods? And could the hoards buried in river valleys, where evidence suggests settlement was also located, be hidden for safekeeping? Or could the two patterns be slight variations (perhaps a local Heacham valley variation) of ritual practices common throughout north-west Norfolk?

Perhaps it is too simplistic to talk in terms of ritual or profane when interpreting the Sedgeford hoard. These theories should not be mutually exclusive – much evidence has shown they were not separate in the Iron Age (Fitzpatrick 1992). The Sedgeford hoard is an example where a specific case can be used to examine more generalised theories. It fits the ritual pattern of deposition proposed above – it was collected together and put into a container. A pit was dug and the hoard was deposited in the ground at a site overlooking the nearby river. The land was not high, just 18m above modern sea-level, fitting the second pattern of deposition in the landscape. But it is unclear whether this pattern represents hoards buried for safekeeping close to settlement, deposits given to a specific god in his or her special place, or a localised form of ritual deposition. The bone container was an unusual feature, perhaps suggesting that the hoard was deposited in unusual circumstances (though bone preservation on the Boneyard site is better than that in most of East Anglia, so bone containers may have been lost elsewhere).

The people who buried the Sedgeford hoard were part of a wider community in north-west Norfolk. This community farmed the landscape. They lived in unenclosed settlements, but they built and maintained complex monumental sites where ritual and votive deposition probably took place. They used similar types of pottery, including forms inspired by Continental examples. They made and used rich metal objects decorated in characteristic local styles. They deposited these metal objects in groups in small pits overlooking water. Despite the strength of this local identity, north-west Norfolk also maintained links with a wider Iron Age world.

BRITAIN AND EUROPE

Contact with the rest of Britain and parts of Europe influenced the way in which the Iron Age people of north-west Norfolk lived (*41*). The series of tracks now known as the Icknield Way linked the region to southern Britain. Despite this, very few southern British objects have been found in north-west Norfolk (Cunliffe 1991). In contrast, torcs made in the region were exported (Northover 1992, 272). A group of Snettisham-style hoards

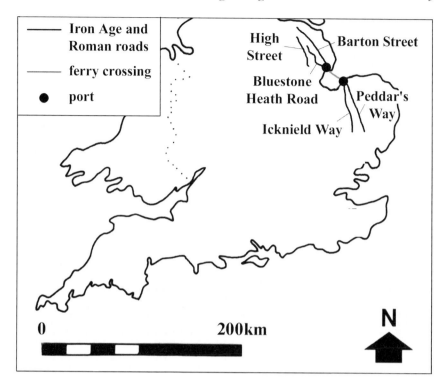

41 How isolated were the Iceni? North-west Norfolk may have been linked to the wider Iron Age world by prehistoric trackways, Roman roads, ferry crossings and international ports. *Illustration by Megan Dennis*

in Ipswich and a scatter of East Anglian coins along the Gipping valley in Suffolk reveal a trade route that must have run down the valley, around the clay uplands of central East Anglia and along the chalk ridge to north-west Norfolk. This path was a major trade route in later periods (Newman 2003) and linked north-west Norfolk to the east coast.

There were also links to the north of England. Prehistoric tracks running across Lincolnshire terminated at The Wash opposite similar paths on the Norfolk side ('the Icknield Way' tracks and the Peddar's Way). This, and a secondary concentration of north-west Norfolk-style objects in Leicestershire and Lincolnshire, strongly implies a sea crossing over The Wash linking the two areas (at a time when the undrained Fens constituted a very formidable barrier to east–west communications overland).

It is likely that ports developed in the Iron Age at the ends of the trackways on either side of The Wash – though no evidence has yet been uncovered.

Imports received here perhaps inspired the imitation Gallo-Belgic pottery found in north-west Norfolk (Flitcroft 2001; Percival 1999). Continental tubular torcs may also have been imported from northern France to be melted down at Snettisham and made into East Anglian types and then exported to other parts of Britain (Northover 1992, 272). Snettisham-style torcs have been found at Ipswich, Suffolk (Owles 1969; Brailsford and Stapley 1972); Ulceby, Humberside (Leeds 1933); and at Shaw Hill, Peebleshire in Scotland (Clarke 1954). Other imports from northern France include the Gallo-Belgic E coins which were deposited in hoards across north-west Norfolk; not only at Sedgeford, but at Buxton-with-Lammas, Fring, Weybourne and Wormegay.

Strong links with the Celtic culture of the Continent are indicated and are responsible for the arrival of the coins of the Sedgeford hoard in the area – though it is curious that, apart from the Gallo-Belgic E staters and some Gallic torcs in the Snettisham hoards, very few actual foreign artefacts have been found, as opposed to local artefacts based on foreign exemplars. Alongside these local copies of foreign exotica, people maintained an indigenous material culture, represented, for instance, by relatively crude handmade ceramics.

Later in the Iron Age, Rome had an increasing influence over people in southern Britain. Some of them adopted rectangular buildings, imported Roman luxuries and made coins directly inspired by Roman *denarii*. In north-west Norfolk, however, Roman influence was weaker. Domestic structures continued to have circular plans until well into the second century AD (Flitcroft 2001) and there is no evidence for the import of Roman luxury goods. Some more subtle changes did occur. However, coins dating to the beginning of the first century AD had Latinised inscriptions (*42*). One of these was *ECEN*. This may be the name the people who lived in East Anglia (and north-west Norfolk) at this time gave themselves. Caesar refers to a tribe called 'the Cenimagni' in the mid first century BC (*The Gallic War*, V, 21), and Tacitus calls them 'the Iceni' when describing the rebellions of 47 BC and AD 60/61 (*The Annals*, 14.31). If those coins are indeed inscribed with the tribal name, they are the only examples of this kind of inscription in Late Iron Age Britain and might demonstrate a strong sense of cultural identity. Finally, after AD 43, a rare type of coin from north-west Norfolk, inscribed *SUBRI ESVPRASTO, ESICO FECIT* (translated as 'under Esuprasto, Esico made me') was based on a Roman-style bust as used on silver denarii.

42 Latin-speaking Iceni? Tribal leaders appear to use increasingly complex Latin inscriptions on their coins. Presumably the early inscription *ECEN* is the tribal name (top). The latest inscription names *ESVPRASTO* as a possible leader and *ESICO* as the minter (bottom). Is *ESVPRASTO* Boudica's husband, the Rome-friendly client king Prasutagus, named as such by Tacitus? *Photographs courtesy of the Celtic Coin Index*

It is clear that these 'Romanising' changes took place within a community that had a strong local identity. They used a characteristic set of objects, some of which were inspired by contacts with other parts of Britain and the Continent. The Sedgeford hoard is one of the earliest examples of this.

CONCLUSIONS

What were the people of Iron Age Sedgeford like? We cannot be certain, but we can propose possibilities.

They lived in small, unenclosed settlements like those excavated at nearby Snettisham. They grew spelt wheat in fields. They used both handmade and wheel-thrown pottery. They used and deposited rich assemblages of metal objects, including the coins of the Sedgeford hoard. They were connected to the wider world of north-west Norfolk by prehistoric tracks and a small river that passed through the valley.

The people of Sedgeford were part of a regional group that used similar objects and constructed comparable sites. Metal items were often collected together in hoards and buried in pits at sites near to, or overlooking water, or at high points in the landscape. The Sedgeford hoard is a further example of this well established pattern. This similarity in ritual implies a people who shared religious beliefs and had a common identity.

There was also communication with a yet wider world. North-west Norfolk was linked to other parts of Britain and to the Continent. Prehistoric trackways linked it with south-east Suffolk and southern Britain generally. Ports and a sea-way across The Wash linked it with northern Britain. These same ports were, no doubt, a link with the Continent. Despite this, the people of the region retained a strong local identity, expressed in characteristic objects, styles of decoration, and the production of coins with a tribal name inscribed on them.

FIVE

INTERPRETATIONS

We have considered the coins, the find-spot and the local environment in other parts of this book. There we concentrated on the particulars, but large questions remain unanswered. Who buried the hoard? When and why? How did the coins get to Sedgeford in the first place? How were they used before burial? In this chapter, with the help of volunteers, academics and archaeologists, we offer possible interpretations. The views expressed vary and sometimes conflict, but rather than choose between them we have left the debate open. Just as our work in the field and on the finds continues, so too does the wider discussion of what it all means.

HOW DID THE COINS GET TO SEDGEFORD?

The coins were made in northern France between 60 and 50 BC, or perhaps a little earlier. So how did they get to Sedgeford? The traditional interpretation is that the coins were produced to pay mercenaries fighting the Romans in the Gallic War. Perhaps a mercenary from Sedgeford was fighting in this war (*colour plate 14*)?

Lloyd Laing, Senior Lecturer, Nottingham University:

> Current around 60-50 BC, the widely accepted view is that the coins were issued in Gaul to pay for support against Caesar in the Gallic War.

Kev Woodward, SHARP volunteer:

> In my opinion, as the coins were all the same type, they are unlikely to have
> been family heirlooms built up over time, but more likely a one-off payment
> for something. As the Gallic wars were being fought at around this time and
> mercenaries were employed to help, the romantic view is that the coins may
> have been connected. In reality we will probably never know.

Recently this interpretation has been questioned.

Jeffrey May, Iron Age specialist and Issue Editor, Current Archaeology:

> Is there really evidence that Gallo-Belgic E coins were brought in by
> mercenaries? I rather think we are dealing with various speculative guesses of
> varying degrees of plausibility.

John Collis, Professor of Archaeology, Sheffield University:

> Incidentally, I do not know of any mentions of the use of British mercenaries
> in the Gallic War (Caesar only mentions help coming from Britain, but he
> is not specific), and he does not mention that any Gallic troops were paid
> (though it may well have happened). So the 'mercenary' interpretation is only
> a hypothesis, and does not in fact explain why there was a continuous flow of
> coins into Britain over nearly a century before Caesar's conquest in Gaul.

How else might the coins have travelled the hundreds of miles from northern Gaul to north-west Norfolk?

Pat Chapman, SHARP finds specialist:

> Could the coins have come with refugees, been used to bribe local support
> for a particular tribal leader, or to support trade? They must have rewarded
> some important project.

John Sills, author of Gaulish and Early British Gold Coinage:

> There is a noticeable tendency for Gallo-Belgic E hoards to be found on
> or near the coast, consistent with the majority having been brought over by

continental Belgae rather than returning British mercenaries. Some hoards may be evidence of coins being traded in quantity at entrepôts for goods and services, while others may be flight hoards deposited by refugees soon after they had landed. ... It is only through the coin evidence that we can test Caesar's statement that the British tribes gave assistance to the Belgae during the Gallic War. Sedgeford reinforces the impression of a large volume of coinage being imported over a short period of time, although the precise mechanisms involved in this huge transfer of wealth are not yet clear.

Lloyd Laing, Senior Lecturer, Nottingham University:

They were not introduced as currency but rather as a 'diplomatic gift'. Was this then a gift to an Icenian leader directly from some resistance leader in Gaul in return for his practical help? This seems unlikely, and given the distribution of hoards of Gallo-Belgic E in the south it seems more probable that this was a gift passed on by a southern chief who had previously supported the Gaulish resistance, but who was now paying off some other debt.

Kev is probably right when he says that we shall never know how the coins reached Sedgeford. It might be important, however, that some of the East Anglian native silver coinages (the 'Bury' types) have very similar designs to silver coins made in the same part of northern France as the Gallo-Belgic E types. Perhaps a small number of refugees moved from northern France to East Anglia after their defeat by the Romans, bringing with them gold and silver coins. They may have deposited some of their gold coins in hoards around the coast, perhaps shortly after they arrived. When they were more settled, they began to make silver coins in similar designs to the ones they used at home (*43*).

HOW WERE THE COINS USED BEFORE THEY WERE BURIED?

The coins may have been paid to mercenaries, but when they were brought to Britain it is unlikely they were used as money. We know that gold coins in Late Iron Age Britain are not generally found on market sites but as individual or multiple finds in isolated locations. The implication is that they were not being used for market exchange but as votive offerings. The gold may have been used as a display of wealth and power.

0   10   20mm

43 Britain imports some Gallic culture. The similarity between coins made in East Anglia (left) and northern France (right) suggest that links were strong between the respective tribal elites. *Photographs courtesy of the Celtic Coin Index and Simone Scheers*

HOW BIG WAS THE HOARD?

We suspect the hoard was bigger than 39 coins. The archaeology of the find-spot shows that the area was disturbed a number of times, and several of the coins were recovered some distance from the hoard pit. So how big was the original hoard? We can guess that the hoard bone may originally have been longer – perhaps almost complete.

Jeffrey May, Iron Age specialist and Issue Editor, Current Archaeology*:*

> If 20 of the 39 coins came from 30 per cent of the length of the bone, presumably the whole hoard could have been contained in the bone if just a knuckle had been sawn off.

Ray Thirkettle, SHARP animal bones specialist:

> No one has suggested the possibility that the rest of the coins may have been deposited *with* the bone rather than *in* it. It would be quite in keeping with the character of a structured deposit to stuff 20 in a bone and place the remainder – God knows how many – just loose in the hole! I tire of folk insisting that the bone was originally in a more complete state. There is absolutely no evidence that this was the case.

Chris Rudd, Celtic coin dealer:

> I think there were originally 40 coins in the hoard: 20 in one humerus and 20
> in its matching twin bone, which got broken at some point and its contents
> dispersed.

This is only speculation. It is unlikely that we will ever know the original
size of the hoard.

WHEN WAS THE HOARD BURIED?

We know the coins were made between 60 and 50 BC, or perhaps slightly
earlier, but how long did it take for them to get to Sedgeford? How long
were they in circulation before burial? Unfortunately these are questions
we cannot answer with certainty. However, the unworn state of most of the
coins suggests that they were not much handled. If we accept that the coins
were brought to the country by sea, the location of the hoard close to the
coast may imply that it was buried soon after the constituent coins arrived
in Britain. Evidence of later Iron Age activity around the find-spot and the
absence of Gallo-Belgic type pottery from the fill of the hoard pit indicates deposition some time before the Roman Conquest. Therefore we can
assume the coins were not in circulation for long and were perhaps buried
in the later first century BC.

WHO BURIED THE HOARD?

This is, again, a difficult question.

Harriet Mackie, SHARP volunteer, aged 8:

> I thought the coins were put in the bone before a soldier went off to war to
> keep them safe, and he must have been killed in the battle and therefore never
> returned to collect his coins. My Grandad said this may have been true as
> they had a lot of wars during this time.

Jean McGinty, SHARP Committee Chairperson:

> The first thought that crossed my mind was of the ingenuity of the person, who had used such an intriguing hiding place. Then, was it hidden by a man or a woman, and how would they have acquired such riches?

The hoard may have been buried by a man or a woman, a warrior or a priest, a native or a refugee. The archaeology of the find-spot does not, unfortunately, help us to identify the individual. The only thing we can say is that the deposit is a rich one and is likely, therefore, to have been owned by a person or persons of high status (or a thief!).

WHY WAS THE HOARD BURIED?

The large number of hoards containing metal objects hidden during the Iron Age has caused many archaeologists to ask why they were deposited in the ground. Until the introduction of the new Treasure Act in 1996 the requirements of medieval treasure trove rules required all hoards to be interpreted as hidden and never retrieved by their owners. Because of this, a number of hoards were interpreted as burials in time of crisis by metalworkers protecting their stashes of raw material or wealthy people their accumulations of bullion. This 'functionalist' approach produced a 'ritual' backlash when the new Treasure Act was introduced in 1996. Suddenly, all hoards were viewed as votive deposits left to appease the gods. Now, several years later, archaeologists are beginning to understand that the modern separation of ritual and functional interpretations may be completely artificial. In the Iron Age, hoards may have been buried for safe-keeping in religious sanctuaries, with prayers to the gods for their safety. Equally, votive treasure may have been regarded as a kind of 'reserve fund', which could be borrowed back from the gods in a crisis. Behaviour like this would not have been confined to Late Iron Age Britain.

Neil Faulkner, SHARP director:

> The Roman dramatist Plautus has a whole play about a miser stashing his pot of gold in the shrine of the Lar (a Roman household god) for safety.

So how do we interpret the Sedgeford hoard? Was it a ritual offering to the Celtic gods (*44*)?

Neil Faulkner, SHARP director:

> Coin expert Jonathan Williams was at the British Museum to receive the Sedgeford hoard when I turned up there to hand it over. I was especially interested in his hunch – supported, I understand, by his colleague J.D. Hill, an Iron Age specialist who has published a British Archaeological Report on the subject – that virtually *all* Iron Age hoards are ritual deposits.

Chris Rudd, Celtic coin dealer:

> If one accepts that the Sedgeford hoard was a ritual deposit – the context strongly suggests that it was – then its container must be of significance. It would have been much easier to bury 39 coins in a leather pouch or little pot. So why take the trouble to cram 20 of them into a hollow cow bone?

Gareth Davies, SHARP director, and Norfolk Archaeological Unit:

> An important ritual element has been observed alongside settlement activity during the Iron Age phases on Boneyard. The clear evidence for ritual acts at certain points in the history of the site does warn us against jumping at purely functionalist or economic interpretations when attempting to explain the hoard.

The proximity of the hoard to the river means that it fits into the local pattern of possible ritual deposition overlooking water. Other hoards of gold coins (including one at Heacham and another at Snettisham) also seem to have been ritually deposited. If we accept this interpretation, what does this tell us about the community carrying out these rituals?

Gareth Davies, SHARP director and Norfolk Archaeological Unit:

> Does the introduction of conspicuous ritual indicate that there had been significant change in the community that lived here? Why would people feel the need to reinforce or legitimise an enclosure or a boundary through the deliberate burial of horses and coins? We can only guess, but the disposal of a valuable asset like a horse in its prime shows that not everyone was living at

44 Interpretation One: The Ritual Theory. *Illustration by Megan Dennis*

subsistence level. If there was a surplus, there was probably a hierarchy, though we do not know the degree of social stratification, nor whether any particular social group was responsible for the rituals. What seems clear is that the ritual areas reveal a community that was still rooted in the land and landscape. The 'ritual zone', with its prominent east–west ditches, is carefully sandwiched between two of the most important landscape zones: fertile and easily tilled farmland to the south, and the fresh water and diverse ecosystem of the valley bottom to the north. Although we do not know the extent of the settlement during the Late Iron Age, the deliberate ritual marking out of the boundary between the upland and the valley bottom suggests widespread occupation and exploitation of the land.

But perhaps we are jumping to conclusions – could the hoard have been hidden to keep it safe? Could the positioning of the cow pelvis over the hoard pit be a marker for someone expecting to come back and retrieve it? Does the absence of other votive offerings in the pit suggest it was being concealed? Perhaps the deposition of the hoard on lower ground compared with other hoards from the area indicates that the hoard was not buried ritually (*45*).

Kev Woodward, SHARP volunteer:

> Theories about why it was buried are broadly split into two camps. There's the ritual theory and the camouflage theory. I belong to the latter, a crafty way to hide your loot – and it worked for two thousand years!

Jean McGinty, SHARP Committee Chairperson:

> Did they plan to return and collect the coins, or did they come back but couldn't find them, or did they never return?

Pat Chapman, SHARP finds specialist:

> I think we should consider the psychological factors. Human instinct, and what would commonly be termed 'gut reaction', together with the basic problems of survival, have not changed over time. The other constant is that gold, probably because it gleams brightly and does not tarnish, has always inspired a sense of awe and value. I believe the original owner's overriding instinct would have been to guard against theft. The use of the bone indicates

45 Interpretation Two: The Security Theory. *Illustration by Megan Dennis*

concealment – someone looking around and choosing something that would not be missed, yet could be expected to last. There is the added bonus that a bone, sealed with mud, would tend to be overlooked by any casual finder, just as it was initially by Kev.

At the moment we do not have enough evidence to prove either of these alternative interpretations. Hopefully, further work on site will clear the matter up. Perhaps, while avoiding the separation of functional and ritual interpretations, we should aim to refine our understanding of exactly how they might have been combined when the hoard was buried.

Neil Faulkner, SHARP director:

> The dichotomy between security hoarding and ritual hoarding is false. Almost certainly, people did deposit more in times of uncertainty, partly for safety, partly to win divine favour and, when they did, they deposited in sanctuaries – the safest places.

John Collis, Professor of Archaeology, Sheffield University:

> As one of the people who started the discussion about contrasts in processes of deposition of gold and bronze coinage in the Iron Age, it is interesting to see better data than I had in the 1970s now coming from excavations and chance finds. However, ritual and domestic activity need not be so completely divorced, and you are dealing with a period when perhaps we see a transition from ritual being carried out mainly on 'domestic' sites (e.g. Danebury) to a period in the early first century BC when specialised sites start appearing (e.g. Hayling Island and Harlow).

Perhaps the refugees from northern France arrived after a hazardous journey fleeing the Roman invaders. They buried their precious gold coins with prayers to their gods thanking them for their safe journey across the channel. But they also intended to return to their gold once they had found a safe and secure place to live, and so placed a cow's pelvis over the hoard pit to make it easier for them to find it again. Perhaps they even chose a local, specialised 'ritual site' for their coins, recognising that locals would be loath to disturb such a place to recover the gold. They never did return, and the hoard lay undisturbed until Anglo-Saxon graves were dug into the pit, and then twenty-first century archaeologists uncovered the bone. But this story, however attractive, is mere speculation.

WHERE DID THEY BURY THE HOARD?

We are still excavating the Iron Age site in which the hoard was buried. We have yet to define its character and chronology.

Jeffrey May, Iron Age specialist and Issue Editor, Current Archaeology:

> I would go easy on the interpretation of the site until much more of it has been excavated. Even then, gullies and ditches are difficult to interpret – as we discovered with two acres of excavation at Iron Age Dragonby in Lincolnshire.

ARE THE HOARD AND THE HORSES LINKED?

The horses found on the site are probably Iron Age, although no radiocarbon dating has yet been done. A small piece of Gallo-Belgic type pottery in the fill of the northern horse burial probably dates it later than the hoard. We have noted that horses were highly prized animals in Late Iron Age East Anglia – perhaps for their importance to the local economy and in warfare. But why were the horses buried on the Boneyard slopes, and was their burial linked to the coin hoard?

Pat Chapman, SHARP finds specialist:

> Has anyone considered that a dead horse is very heavy and, even today, is often buried in a hole next to where it died? The fact that the front legs were bent upwards supports this interpretation.

Chris Rudd, Celtic coin dealer:

> It shouldn't surprise anyone that horses were buried at Sedgeford. Norfolk and north Suffolk have a long and strong tradition of horse breeding that dates from the Late Iron Age (maybe much earlier) to the present day (e.g.

at Newmarket). That's why more horse gear, such as terret rings and strap junctions, have been found in these counties than anywhere else in Britain. Even the tribal name itself, Eceni (as on coins) or Iceni (as in Latin historical writings), may mean 'horse people'. Bruce Robinson and the late Tony Gregory said: 'It is interesting that the only survival of the name of the tribe, apart from place names, is the adjective 'ickeny' which was used in the dialect of Norfolk and Lincolnshire for things awkward and difficult to manage, and particularly for difficult horses. Could this have been a memory of the Iceni as horse dealers and breeders?'(1987, 17).

Horses were a feature of life, not only in Late Iron Age East Anglia. Some interesting parallels are being excavated on the continent.

John Collis, Professor of Archaeology, Sheffield University:

Interesting about the horses – quite a lot have been coming up from the Auvergne region in France. The *Daily Mail* picked up on one find with eight horses and eight men from Gondole, but a more recent excavation produced 57 horses, in several cases laid out together in pits (I think up to 14 horses per pit). I believe, incidentally, that this is a site with evidence of domestic activity.

WHY WERE HORSES BURIED?

James Riches, SHARP volunteer:

Was this a ritual burial? Could this horse have drawn a chariot? Was it just some old nag thrown into a convenient pit? Who knows? I would like to think that it was a chariot war-horse reverently buried upon the death of its master or mistress.

Jeffrey May, Iron Age specialist and Issue Editor, Current Archaeology:

As for animal burials, are they ritual, or diseased animals, or a favourite pony? Plenty of guesses can be made, according to our currently fashionable views of Iron Age society, but real evidence is another matter.

We hope that closer analysis of the skeletons may reveal how the horses died. This might give us a clue about whether they were sacrificed (as the acute angle of the neck and the apparent hole in the skull of the northern horse suggest), or died naturally.

HOW IMPORTANT AND VALUABLE IS THE HOARD?

The hoard was recovered from a site with well-preserved remains during a controlled excavation. This means that a lot of information about context is available – with more to come.

Philip de Jersey, Research Assistant, Keeper of the Celtic Coin Index, Institute of Archaeology, Oxford University:

> While the coins are beautiful and have an obvious intrinsic interest, to my mind it is the context of the hoard and the manner in which it was recovered that are the most significant features of this discovery. Only a handful of Iron Age coin hoards have been recovered archaeologically, with due attention paid to the surroundings of the find, and this provides us with an enormous opportunity to gain further information about the coins themselves, and to speculate on the reasons why they were buried.

John Davies, Chief Curator, Norwich Castle Museum:

> Very few hoards are discovered during research excavation. This makes the recovery of the Sedgeford deposit different and special. In fact, very few coin hoards are ever excavated. The majority have turned up by chance, and a lot of information has been lost due to the method of recovery. This is one area of archaeology where a huge amount of potential information has been lost over the years. It would be so good if finders would inform archaeologists as soon as they suspect the presence of a hoard, so that the contents can be extracted under scientific conditions, taking account of the context and sequence of deposition. Note the high level of information recovered when the Snettisham torc hoards were properly excavated.

46 Detecting the past. The Sedgeford project uses metal detectors routinely as a survey technique. The expertise of experienced metal-detectorists is in these instances invaluable. *Photograph by Jim Reid*

Chris Rudd, Celtic coin dealer:

> The fact that the Sedgeford hoard was unearthed during a research dig is of crucial importance, because it permits a more sensitive analysis of the circumstances of deposition. A comparison with the Market Harborough hoard immediately springs to mind, because much of this hoard was recovered by archaeological excavation. The sad difference is this: since the Market Harborough hoard was publicised on TV, the location of the site was instantly recognised by 'nighthawks', who have been raping it ever since. It is rumoured that hundreds more Iron Age coins have been illicitly taken from the site; most of these coins will never be recorded and the numismatic picture will therefore remain incomplete.

Metal-detectorists often get a bad press from archaeologists (*46*). The Sedgeford hoard is an important example of how archaeologists and detec-torists can work together to learn more about the past.

Philip de Jersey, Research Assistant, Keeper of the Celtic Coin Index, Institute of Archaeology, Oxford University:

> It's all the more satisfying that the discovery of the hoard combined the skills of metal-detectorists with those of archaeologists; and particularly appropriate that this should take place in Norfolk, where co-operation between the detecting and archaeological fraternities has existed since long before the introduction of the Portable Antiquities Scheme. The discovery of the Sedgeford hoard is an excellent demonstration of how both detectorists and archaeologists can benefit when they work together.

John Davies, Chief Curator, Norwich Castle Museum:

> I believe that it is very important for metal-detectorists and archaeologists to
> work together. A vast amount of important information has been recovered
> from the soil of Norfolk this way, and this has transformed our understanding
> of all archaeological periods and our knowledge of artefacts (including coins)
> of all periods. Metal-detecting is a genuine hobby enjoyed by enthusiasts. It
> will continue whether or not archaeologists work with them. It is far better
> to work together. Also, metal-detectors can be useful tools when used on
> excavations or surveys. Their use is a real skill. The recovery rate when used by
> an amateur (such as an inexperienced archaeological excavator) is much less
> than when used by an experienced detectorist who has a flair for the work.
> So it is also useful to work with experienced detectorists in an archaeological
> situation.

The community archaeology aspects of the SHARP project also make the
discovery and subsequent handling of the hoard unusual and important.

Kev Woodward, SHARP volunteer:

> The way the many specialists involved recorded every detail as a contribution
> towards an overall picture was a privilege to witness. I, as an amateur
> archaeologist, was not made to feel an outsider; in fact, the opposite was
> true. The greatest honour was being given the opportunity to excavate the
> contents of the bone: no greater trust could have been shown. SHARP is not
> hierarchical; it is public access to archaeology in its nicest form.

Jane Southgate, SHARP volunteer:

> What really impressed me at the time was the way the discovery was handled.
> Everyone was kept fully informed as events unfolded; opinions were actively
> sought and matters openly discussed. It proved to me that community
> archaeology, when well-organised and led, can be of great benefit to the
> discipline and its practitioners whilst still providing an active and fulfilling
> learning experience for 'amateurs'.

Many people are interested in the modern monetary value of the hoard.
For the archaeologists who have worked with the hoard, however, this is

unimportant. The chance to find out more about the people who lived in the past, present it to the public and give them a chance to connect with the material is what gives us a buzz. Perhaps in the end the Sedgeford hoard is important because it has touched so many people's lives. Each of these people's reactions to and interpretations of the hoard are relevant. They are personal engagements with the past. They reflect their intellectual excitement. Hardened archaeologists, trained to deal strictly with evidence, came to sense the importance of this.

Gareth Davies, SHARP director and Norfolk Archaeological Unit:

> The argument about ritual worried me at first. I was inclined to stress the 'normal' domestic aspects of the site. There seemed too much wild speculation. Then my view changed. Though I think Jeffrey May is correct to say we should hold back on interpretation until more of the site is excavated, I realised we were in a situation where interpretation cannot be held back. The many reflections on the hoard help interpret it far better than any one written edict issued by the Sedgeford project. Some will appear laughable in a few years, but this publication will fossilise them, and thus preserve them as part of the record of the whole history of the Sedgeford hoard. Many people with vastly different outlooks, knowledge bases and agendas have interpreted the Sedgeford hoard. It, therefore, for better or worse, has come to mean many different things to many different people.

WHAT HAPPENS NOW?

King's Lynn Museum has acquired the hoard. It will be on display when the museum reopens, after refurbishment, in Spring 2006. Meanwhile SHARP continues to investigate the history and archaeology of human activity in Sedgeford, from earliest times to the present day, with the help of the local community and a large team of volunteers. The story of occupation in the area is far from complete. We are looking forward to spending many more years digging for answers.

SIX

TREASURE AND THE COMMUNITY

What is treasure? Who defines it and controls its fate? What is treasure's relationship with the rest of the archaeological record? What does treasure mean to society as a whole? The discovery of a hoard of 39 gold staters in the context of a research project committed to 'democratic archaeology' has raised interesting issues.

Gold is seductive. The astonishing thing about gold is that it is stunningly beautiful the moment you uncover it. Silver looks purple-grey, bronze goes green and iron turns into shapeless rusty lumps. Not so gold: there is no corrosion, no discoloration, just the same brilliant yellow gleam it had when its owner last saw it hundreds or even thousands of years before. It worked its charm on our excavators. 'This was something special,' said Terry Baxter, the site supervisor on the spot. 'No-one there was unaffected by it. How could we not be?' When Charlotte Burrill, another supervisor, brought the cow bone with two gold staters visible inside the broken end of the shaft into the Finds Hut, 'her hands were trembling and she looked quite white with shock'. When volunteers working at the wet-sieving station discovered two more staters in the spoil from the pit, there were 'screams of delight'. 'Being present when the hoard was found and actually finding a gold coin myself,' recalls volunteer Rebecca Ferrugia, 'was truly a fantastic experience. Even more thrilling is knowing that we were the first people to hold these coins since they were last buried. This is such a rare and exciting experience, and it is one that I will always treasure.' Kev Woodward, the finder of the hoard, excavating the interior of the cow bone two days later, 'revealed a beautiful sight I hope never to forget: at least eight gold staters stacked one on top of the other and all shining back at me like they were made the day before.' A veteran radio reporter from BBC Norfolk was covering the event live. When Kevin dropped a gold stater he had just excavated from his tweezers into the palm of her hand, making her the first person to hold it for 2,000 years, she was, despite a radio audience of thousands, momentarily speechless. Such is the power of gold.

SHARP is a collective of researchers rooted in a local community. Rising from the earth into this context, the gold at first belonged to all – to be seen, to be held, to fascinate, to seduce. Then, by the rules under which we live, it was bound to pass on, out of the hands of the people who delivered it into a morally murkier world of treasure law and heritage politics.

It might, indeed, have moved on faster had not the democratic ethos that pervades the project slowed it down. As soon as the news broke, the authorities made known their view that the bone should be excavated at the British Museum. They were less quick to offer assistance in establishing whether this would be necessary: the Norfolk museums' conservation department had 'no contract with the project' and would therefore have to charge for any work done; but, in any case, they were too busy at the time to take it on. It was a local hospital that took the X-rays – free of charge, within the hour. Once it was clear that the contents of the bone were not corroded – so no tricky conservation would be required – the regular SHARP volunteer who had found the hoard was invited to excavate it, and the work was carried out immediately on site.

These two decisions confounded expectations. 'I thought this was going to be whisked away to the British Museum,' Kev told a local newspaper reporter, 'and to be asked to do it is a great honour. I'm quite humbled really – you're actually handling them for the first time in 2,000 years. This is the good thing about SHARP: that it is not hierarchical; it's public access in its nicest form.' Both decisions appear to have had unanimous support among the hundred or so people on site or otherwise closely associated with the project. The hoard, therefore, was excavated and recorded by the research team that discovered it – not by distant 'experts' who specialise in 'treasure' – and it has been interpreted in the context of all the other information gathered by that same research team. This report is the result. The fact that it has been published so quickly is testament to the success of community archaeology and the enthusiasm and dedication of those involved.

After excavation, the gold entered the treasure process. This is now governed by a new Treasure Act which came into force in September 1997 (with modifications effective from January 2003). By this law, the following objects are deemed treasure:

1 All coins from the same find (two or more) provided they are at least 300 years old when found. If they contain less than 10 per cent gold or silver, there must be at least 10 of them.

2 All prehistoric base-metal objects from the same find (two or more). All finds (one or more) at least 300 years old and containing 10 per cent or more gold or silver.

3 Any object, whatever it is made of, found in the same place as (or having previously been together with) another object that is treasure.

The new law replaced the medieval law of Treasure Trove, where the definition of treasure had depended, absurdly, on the presumed intentions of the original hoarder. The new law, in effect, encompasses all portable antiquities recovered from the ground likely to have a significant commercial value – irrespective of the reasons for deposition – and provides finders with an incentive to report such discoveries by offering the current market price as a reward should a museum exercise its right to purchase.

The result has been a roughly tenfold increase in the reporting of treasure finds (DCMS 2003, 2), and the new law must therefore be considered, in the circumstances, a necessary reform. It does remain a compromise between three, partly contradictory, aspects of treasure in modern society: commercial value, antiquarian interest, and heritage management. The original thirteenth-century law of Treasure Trove vested ownership in the king (presumably, in consequence, reporting of chance finds was not good). In 1886, by which time antiquarian values had come to outweigh commercial ones, the law was modified to encourage reporting by paying rewards to finders. Today, when most treasure finds are made by metal-detectorists, it is common for rewards to be split, on the basis of prior agreement, between finders and landowners. The state, in its capacity as guardian of national heritage, is the arbiter of the process. Treasure is defined as such by coroners' courts acting on the advice of the British Museum (in the case of discoveries in England). Market values are assigned by an official body known as the

'Treasure Valuation Committee', and it is the British Museum, followed by other public museums, that has a right of acquisition (Hobbs 2003, 10-28). Treasure law, in short, is a compromise between profit, research and state authority.

Hierarchies structure the way archaeologists work. More specifically, they determine who has the power of decision, and who performs what tasks within the discipline. Though field archaeology is a skilled occupation and has evolved into a graduate-entry profession, employed archaeologists are ranked in a hierarchy. In theory, their position in the hierarchy determines the difficulty of the tasks they perform, the degree of control they have over their work, the responsibility they hold and the level of reward they receive. Also, in theory, an archaeologist is ranked in relation to her/his qualifications, experience, skills, general competence and past achievements. This organisation of work mirrors that in society at large: broadly, there is a division of labour not only between occupations but also within them, such that skill and control are unequally distributed in work processes. In the case of archaeology, moreover, because it attracts large numbers of volunteer workers, the hierarchical organisation of work acquires in this case an extra dimension: the relative ranking of 'amateurs' and 'professionals'. Archaeological activities range from those which it is considered anyone can do, such as fieldwalking, to those considered appropriate only for 'professionals', such as excavation, to those reserved for 'specialists', such as work on rare and high-value items (like treasure).

One example is the official reaction to the discovery of the Sedgeford hoard discussed above. Let us consider another to strengthen the point. It concerns Basil Brown, the excavator whose brilliance recovered the shape of the ship buried under Mound One at Sutton Hoo in 1939. Because he was a self-taught local archaeologist, when the burial chamber within the ship was found to be intact and likely to contain rich grave-goods, he was, on the advice of the British Museum, replaced as project director by a Cambridge don (Carver 1998, 2-24). The digging of treasure required an academic, a university man; perhaps, indeed, in the 1930s anyway, 'a gentleman'. The advice given to us in the summer of 2003 was no different in principle: there was the implication, first, that treasure has a higher value than other material, not only commercially *but also archaeologically*, and second, that it should therefore be processed by more highly qualified 'specialists'.

Let us consider the implications of this approach. Which mattered more in 1939, the ship or the grave-goods? The question is (a) pointless and

(b) impossible to answer. Both ship and grave-goods were of enormous archaeological significance. Which was easier to excavate? The grave-goods, without doubt, since their recovery required mainly patience and care, whereas the ship demanded a radically new excavation strategy to recover its form from lines of rusty rivets and stains in the sand. In relation to the Sedgeford hoard, we might ask whether coins or context matter more, but again the question would be absurd: they are two aspects of a single investigation, and both should be recovered as fully as possible. It makes no sense to take any part of an archaeological sequence out of the integrated research programme in which it occurs. The job of 'specialists', therefore, should not be to usurp other researchers, but to provide the advice and support needed to facilitate their work. That this is not the instinctive response of heritage authorities may have more to do with the politics of bureaucratic hierarchies than with the exigencies of research. These hierarchies are echoed in the official proposed scheme of work for the hoard. The work was to be fragmented, each task given a rank order of importance, and archaeologists allocated to tasks according to seniority and ostensible expertise.

Michael Shanks and Randall McGuire have criticised this approach to archaeology by counterposing the idea of archaeology as a 'craft' (1996). 'The idea of archaeology as a craft,' they explain, 'challenges the separation of reasoning and execution that characterises the field today.' Craft, for them, implies a comprehensive creative, in which 'purpose' (research aims and relevance to society), 'viability' (the material remains and the methods used to explore them) and 'expression' (the many personal satisfactions to be had from archaeological work) interact.

At Sedgeford we attempt to realise this ideal in practice: that is, to make archaeology an integrated activity in which each practitioner comes to share in 'reasoning and execution', such that the discipline becomes 'a unified practice of hand, heart and mind'. We do this knowing that our practice constitutes an implicit critique of the norm, where there is fragmentation of labour, a separation of control from execution, and the ranking of people in rigid occupational hierarchies. SHARP represents a practical attempt to deconstruct hierarchies in order to release the creative energies they hold in check. The discovery of the hoard, by involving SHARP in close interaction with external archaeological authority, highlighted the contrast between what have elsewhere been called 'archaeology from above' and 'archaeology from below' (Faulkner 2000).

We have been criticised at SHARP for creating a rural idyll – a relaxed summer research dig where we are accountable to no-one but ourselves and can engage in self-indulgent experiments in building democracy in a field (*pers. comm.*). The real world, we are told, is quite different, and what we do at SHARP has no relevance there. The answer to this is simple enough: the 'real' world is not a given; it is something made and continually re-made by human beings. One way of exploring alternatives is to conduct experiments where we can demonstrate that these alternatives exist.

Sedgeford aspires to show in practice that work need not be fragmented, hierarchical and exclusive; that it might, on the contrary, be creative, empowering and satisfying. We can illustrate this with some examples of people's interactions with the treasure in August 2003. These interactions arose because the treasure was not 'whisked away to the British Museum', but was excavated, analysed, displayed and discussed as part of the project which found it. For many days after its discovery, it remained an integral part of SHARP.

For the leading archaeologists, especially Megan Dennis, who co-ordinated the post-excavation project, Gareth Davies, who supervised the excavation of the hoard pit, and Chris Mackie, who organised the media coverage, work on the Sedgeford hoard was an opportunity to develop their skills to higher levels. 'I enjoyed thriving in a crisis,' recalls Gareth. 'I saw the hoard pit as an entity that had to be fully tackled. Although it now had to be done properly under my supervision that still meant involving as many of the volunteers as possible. Over the first two days after the find, I can honestly say I worked harder and longer than at any other time during my archaeological career of eight years.' Megan was also stretched but exhilarated: 'The nerves began to vanish after a few days – we had completed an excellent job with the help of the local pharmacist, the X-ray department of a local hospital, an artist, several photographers, local students, an RAF technician and the support of an amazing team.' Chris's wife Mary records her husband's state of mind when he arrived home with the hoard in his possession on the day of discovery: 'He showed us the bone – and the two shiny gold coins that were visible embedded in the 2,000-year-old mud that filled it. I have seldom seen him so excited. His mood infected all of us as he told us about his day … The treasure resided in our bungalow that night (and the next). Chris claims he hardly slept a wink.'

Other supervisors and volunteers also had important roles and gained experience in the excavation, recording and analysis of special deposits – some on site, some in the improvised lab where the bone was excavated.

Everyone, moreover, was able to share something of the excitement. The discussion about how the discovery was to be recorded, displayed and interpreted was held in public, and, once the coins had been excavated, catalogued and bagged, the hoard was passed round for everyone on site to see and hold. The discovery reached out and touched the local community – the two hospital radiologists who took the X-rays, the local pharmacist who weighed the coins and then the hundreds who came to see the hoard, many queuing in the sun for up to 20 minutes without complaint, chatting happily together, firing questions at SHARP volunteers near at hand, waiting to pay homage to the treasure and thrilled that it was still there to be seen in the field from which it had been dug three days before.

The recovery and investigation of the Sedgeford hoard was an example of archaeology as craft. The process was rooted in the community – the discovery remained embedded in its own contemporary context. All parts of the process remained joined together as the on-going work of a single team: recovery from the ground; investigation of context; excavation of the bone; analysis of the coins; discussion about their meaning and presentation to the public. Through their ownership of the project and the exercise of control and creativity that it afforded, the archaeologists involved were able to demonstrate and increase their skill, knowledge and confidence.

We have demonstrated that another way of doing archaeology is possible. Perhaps we have also shown that another way of organising work generally is possible: that it can be collective and democratic, empowering and enriching. Perhaps, indeed, we have shown that, to use a slogan of our age, 'another world is possible'.

REFERENCES

Allen, D.F., 1980, *Coins of the Ancient Celts*, Edinburgh, Edinburgh University Press.

Brailsford, J.W. and Stapley, J.E., 1972, 'The Ipswich torcs', in *Proceedings of the Prehistoric Society*, 38, 219-234.

Burnett, A.M. and Cowell, M.R., 1988, 'Celtic Coinage in Britain II', in *British Numismatic Journal*, 58, 1-10.

Carver, M., 1998, *Sutton Hoo: burial ground of kings?*, London, British Museum Press.

Chadburn, A., 1990, 'A hoard of Iron Age silver coins from Fring, Norfolk and some observations on the Icenian coin series', in *British Numismatic Journal* 60, 1-12.

Chadburn, A. and Gurney, D., 1991, 'The Fring coin hoard', in *Norfolk Archaeology*, 41, 2, 218-225.

Clarke, R.R., 1951, 'A hoard of metalwork of the Early Iron Age from Ringstead, Norfolk', in *Proceedings of the Prehistoric Society*, 17, 514-525.

— 1954, 'The Early Iron Age treasure from Snettisham, Norfolk', in *Proceedings of the Prehistoric Society*, New Series 20, 1, 27-87.

Crabtree, P.J., 1989, *West Stow, Early Anglo-Saxon Husbandry*, East Anglian Archaeology Report No. 47, Ipswich, Suffolk County Planning Dept.

Creighton, J., 2000, *Coins and Power in Late Iron Age Britain*, Cambridge, Cambridge University Press.

Cunliffe, B., 1991, *Iron Age Communities in Britain*, London, Routledge.

Davies, J.A., 1996, 'Where eagles dare: the Iron Age in Norfolk', in *Proceedings of the Prehistoric Society*, 62, 63-93.

—1999, 'Patterns, power and political progress in Late Iron Age Norfolk', in Davies, J.A. and Williamson, T. (eds), *Land of the Iceni: the Iron Age of northern East Anglia*, Norwich, Centre of East Anglian Studies, University of East Anglia, 14-41.

DCMS (Department for Culture, Media and Sport), 2003, *Treasure Annual Report 2001*, London, DCMS.

de Jersey, P., 1996, *Celtic Coinage in Britain*, Princes Risborough, Shire Archaeology.

Dennis, M., forthcoming, 'Late Iron Age and Early Roman East Anglian silver hoards', in Wellington, I. and Davies, M. (eds), *New Research on the Iron Age*, British

Archaeological Reports, British Series.

Faulkner, N., 2000, 'Archaeology from below', in *Public Archaeology*, 1, 1, 21-33.

Fitzpatrick, A.P., 1992, 'The Snettisham, Norfolk, hoards of Iron Age torques: sacred or profane?', in *Antiquity*, 66, 395-8.

Flitcroft, M., 2001, *Excavation of a Romano-British Settlement on the Snettisham Bypass, 1989*, Norfolk, Archaeology and Environment Division, Norfolk Museums and Archaeology Service.

Gregory, T., 1991, *Excavations in Thetford, 1980-82, Fison Way*, East Anglian Archaeology Report 53.

Harrison, S., 2002, 'Open fields and earlier landscapes: six parishes in south-east Cambridgeshire', in *Landscapes*, 3, 1, 35-54.

Haselgrove, C., 1984, 'Warfare and its aftermath as reflected in the precious metal coinage of Belgic Gaul', in *Oxford Journal of Archaeology*, 3, 1, 81-99.

— 1999, 'The development of Iron Age coinage in Belgic Gaul', in *Numismatic Chronicle*, 159, 111-168.

Hesse, M., 1992, 'Fields, tracks and boundaries in the Creakes, North Norfolk', in *Norfolk Archaeology*, 41, 305-324.

Hill, J.D., 1999, 'Settlement, landscape and regionality: Norfolk and Suffolk in the pre-Roman Iron Age of Britain and beyond', in Davies, J.A. and Williamson, T. (eds), *Land of the Iceni: the Iron Age of northern East Anglia*, Norwich, Centre of East Anglian Studies, University of East Anglia, 185-207.

Hinton, D., 1997, 'The Scole-Dickleburgh field system examined', in *Landscape History*, 19, 1-12.

Hobbs, R., 2003, *Treasure: finding our past*, London, The British Museum Press.

Hutcheson, N., 2001, 'Late Iron Age horse equipment from Norfolk: colouring in the Iceni', unpublished conference paper.

— 2003, 'Material culture in the landscape: a new approach to the Snettisham hoards', in Humphreys, J. (ed) *Re-searching the Iron Age*, Leicester, University of Leicester, School of Archaeology and Ancient History, Leicester Archaeology Monographs 11.

— 2004, *Later Iron Age Norfolk: metalwork, landscape and society*, Oxford, British Archaeological Reports, British Series 361.

Ingleby, H., 1925, *The Charm of a Village: Sedgeford*, London.

Leeds, E.T., 1933, 'Torcs of the Early Iron Age', in *The Antiquaries Journal*, 13, 4, 466-468.

Lewton-Braine, C.H., 1953, 'Eight Iron Age pits from south of Caley Mill, Heacham', unpublished site notebook, Norfolk Historic Environment Records Office.

Lyons, A., 1996, 'The Late Iron Age to Early Roman transition in Norfolk', unpublished paper to the Study Group for Roman Pottery.

Millet, M., 1985, 'Field survey calibration, a contribution.', in Haselgrove, C., Millet, M. and Smith, I. (eds), *Archaeology from the Ploughsoil: studies in the collection of field survey data*, Department of Archaeology, University of Sheffield.

Newman, J., 2003, 'Exceptional Finds, Exceptional Sites? Barham and Coddenham, Suffolk: markets', in Pestell, T. and Ulmschneider, K. (eds), *Early Medieval Europe: trading and 'productive' sites, 650-850*, Macclesfield, Windgather Press, 97-109.

Northover, J.P., 1992, 'Material issues in the Celtic coinage', in Mays, M. (ed), *Celtic*

Coinage: Britain and beyond, Oxford, British Archaeological Reports 222, 235-299.

Oosthuizen, S., 1998, 'Prehistoric fields into medieval furlongs?: evidence from Caxton, south Cambridgeshire', in *Proceedings of the Cambridgeshire Antiquarian Society*, 86, 145-52.
— 2003, 'The roots of the common fields: linking prehistoric and Medieval field systems in West Cambridgeshire', in *Landscapes*, 4, 1, 40-64.
Owles, E., 1969, 'The Ipswich gold torcs', in *Antiquity*, 43, 208-212.

Palk, N.A., 1984, *Iron Age Bridle Bits from Britain*, Edinburgh, University of Edinburgh, Department of Archaeology Occasional Paper 10.
Percival, S., 1995, 'Iron Age pottery from two pits at Fincham, Norfolk', in *Norfolk Archaeology*, 52, 2, 215-217.
— 1999, 'Iron Age pottery in Norfolk', in Davies, J.A. and Williamson, T. (eds), *Land of the Iceni: the Iron Age of northern East Anglia*, Norwich, Centre of East Anglian Studies, University of East Anglia, 173-185.
Petch, J.A., 1924, *Early Man in the District of Huddersfield*, Huddersfield.

Robinson, B. and Gregory, T., 1987, *Celtic Fire and Roman Rule: Norfolk Origins 3*, Norfolk, Poppyland Publishing.

Scheers, S., 1977, *Traite de numismatique celtique II: La Gaule Belgique*, Paris, Annales Litéraires de l'Universitairé de Besançon, 195.
Shanks, M. and McGuire, R., 1996, 'The craft of archaeology', in *American Antiquity*, 61(1), 75-88.
Slowikowski, A.M., 1995, 'The greatest depository of archaeological material: the role of pottery in ploughzone archaeology', in Sheperd, L. (ed), *Interpreting Stratigraphy 1995*, Norwich.
Stead, I.M., 1991, 'The Snettisham treasure: excavations in 1990', in *Antiquity*, 65, 447-65.
— 1995, 'Die Schatzfunde von Snettisham', in Haffner, A. (ed), *Heiligtümer und opferkulte der kelten*, special issue of *Archäologie in Deutschland*, Stuttgart.
— 1998, *The Salisbury Hoard*, Stroud, Tempus.

Talbot, J., forthcoming, 'Early East Anglian Iron Age coins', in de Jersey, P. (ed), *New Research in Celtic Coins*, Oxford, British Archaeological Reports, British Series.

Williamson, T., 1987, 'Early co-axial field systems on the East Anglian boulder clays', in *Proceedings of the Prehistoric Society*, 53, 419-31.
— 1998 'The Scole-Dickleburgh field system re-visited', in *Landscape History*, 20, 19-28.
— 2000, *The Origins of Hertfordshire*, Manchester, Manchester University Press.
— 2003, 'The 'Scole-Dickleburgh field system' in context: co-axial landscapes in Norfolk and beyond', in *The Annual*, 12, 13-25.

Classical Sources

De Bello Gallico
Edwards, H.J. (trans), 1917, *Caesar: the Gallic War*, London, Harvard University Press.

Annals
Church, A.J. (trans), 1877, *Annals of Tacitus*, London, Macmillan.